THE NONPROFITS'
GUIDE TO
THE POWER OF
APPRECIATIVE INQUIRY

Authors:

Carolyn J. Miller
Cristina R. Aguilar
Linda Maslowski
Donna McDaniel
Michael J. Mantel

Published by: Community Development Institute
9745 E. Hampden Suite 310
Denver, CO 80231
303-369-5959

Printed in the United States of America
ISBN 0-9761843-0-3

The Nonprofits' Guide to the Power of Appreciative inquiry

DEDICATION

This book is fondly dedicated to our dear colleague, friend and primary editor, Jeffrey Fisher, who passed away in his sleep on May 5, 2004. The idea for this book originally came from Jeffrey in the summer of 2003. He was and continues to be for many of us, a powerful inspiration for future possibilities. Based on his work with Landmark Education, he continually reminded us that anything we want to create is only a few conversations away.

ACKNOWLEDGEMENTS

The authors are indebted to the groundbreaking work of the pioneers who fashioned Appreciative Inquiry into a potent process for organizational change and development. David L. Cooperrider, Diana Whitney, Jim Ludema, Amanda Trosten-Bloom and *many others who have brought AI into our businesses, government agencies, churches, nonprofits and schools.* We also wish to thank the following people who have contributed to this book: Sandy Hill-Binkley, Kris Black, Jill Bryan, Graig Casada, Jana Cook, Grace Hardy, Deb Hinrichs, Royal Johnson, Lisa Main, Mike Miller, Brie Reimann, Nila Rinehart, Belinda Rinker, Ted Sanquist, Leslie Sherlock, Larry Siroshton, Patti Smith, Deborah Mabry-Strong, Kathy Turner, Paul Villar, Tish Wilson, Peter Maslowski, Karen Stefaniak, Susan Wood, Alice Eberhart-Wright and University of Kentucky Hospital/Children's Hospital.

I believe we can change the world if we start listening to one another again. Simple, honest, human conversation. Not mediation, negotiation, problem-solving, debate, or public meetings. Simple, truthful conversation where we each have a chance to speak, we each feel heard and we each listen well.

—Margaret J. Wheatley,
<u>Turning To One Another</u>

TABLE OF CONTENTS

Human beings and organizational systems tend to grow toward what they persistently study and ask questions about.

Promoting Positive Parenting Through Positive Interactions

A child and family program serving infants and teen mothers in Kansas was disheartened by the lack of involvement of the mothers with their infants and the poor attendance at group parent meetings. The program employed numerous techniques to better involve parents, all of which failed. Alice Eberhart-Wright, a consultant the program engaged, has been an advocate for identifying and building on strengths during her long and varied professional career. She began by visiting each home, getting to know the mothers and getting permission to videotape them interacting with their infants, a process Alice calls "Focus and Reflect." During the videotaping, Alice made only positive comments: "It's so wonderful the way you are talking to your child. I can see that she is really looking at you and following your voice and movements." Progressively she engaged the mothers in conversations beginning with positive questions: "What is something you remember from your childhood that was so much fun for you?"

After videotaping, Alice explained to the parents that she would be editing the tapes, highlighting positive interactions between mothers and their children and showing them at the next group parent meeting. She expressed her gratitude for the positive ways of interacting with infants the mothers had provided and indicated that all parents could learn from watching one another and talking among themselves.

A month passed. Notices went out for the next parent meeting reminding parents that they would view their videos. Guess what? Nearly all the mothers showed up. They were eager to see themselves in the video, glowed in the praise of others, became engaged in conversation, began developing relationships and learned valuable skills from one another. And they were eager for more visits and more parent meetings.

Alice trained the staff on the techniques of using positive questions, positive interaction and videotaping. The staff now reports continued success in parent meeting attendance and more importantly, in positive parent/child interactions.

The Binding Language of Values

The staff of a California nonprofit which consisted of native speakers of Spanish, Russian and English was rife with grievance, distrust, blame and confrontation. The authors' nonprofit corporation, Community Development Institute (CDI), was brought in to manage and revitalize the organization. As a first step in rebuilding enthusiasm for and pride in the organization's mission and fostering collaboration, we identified a need to draw out and build on the organization's core values.

Convening an all-staff meeting — 100 people, including administrators to custodians — was the first step in establishing a new, more positive tone and rededication to the inherent values of the nonprofit service provider. The assembly's pervasive mood was glum, guarded and skeptical. Participants sat with arms crossed, talking in hushed tones with their neighbors, not looking up to the front of the room. They filled seats from the back rows forward, leaving empty chairs, like a no-man's-land, between linguistic factions. Mistrust and resignation were palpable. To add to the awkwardness, translators were required, so that every sentence had to be repeated twice — a process that tried the patience of an already impatient audience.

We designed the meeting using the Appreciative Inquiry (AI) technique asking positive questions to elicit values through stories told in interviews. Participants conducted reciprocal interviews with one other person in the room. The basic instructions were: "Listen attentively; don't interrupt or get distracted by thinking about what *you're* going to say and don't take over the conversation. Everyone will be

9

interviewed; you'll all have an opportunity to be heard." Participants were sitting with people they knew, so grumbling and sour looks accompanied the instructions to pair up with someone they did not work with on a daily basis but who spoke their language.

Two questions comprised the interview. The first focused on a high point, a peak experience interviewees had while working in this organization or another. Interviewees told a story of their experience: who was involved, how it happened, what made it a peak experience. The second question asked them to talk about the positive contributions this organization can make in its community when functioning at its best.

Interviewing began quietly but soon became louder and very animated. Positive energy permeated the room. Most participants got caught up in listening and telling stories. Their body language shifted — they relaxed, uncrossed their arms and leaned in to one another.

After the interviews, participants retold their partners' stories, which they did in three languages, translated twice, for the benefit of a now rapt and appreciative audience. Following the storytelling, the facilitator guided the group in extrapolating the values inherent in the stories. Inscribed inside a large heart on a flipchart, the values became a symbol of the organization's core principles and now hangs in the administrative offices. Formerly deeply divided staff members began a process of collaboration and agreement leading to a productive and effective working environment.

Now enthusiastic converts to an outlook of positive intent, management initiated AI processes throughout individual departments. The result is a noticeable boost in morale, unprecedented cooperation among departments and organization wide performance improvement, as measured internally by self-assessments and externally by renewed invitations to collaborate with other community organizations.

Nursing Excellence — The UK Way:
Celebrating Nursing at its Best

It started when one woman, a dedicated nurse named Karen who received a copy of Thin Book of Appreciative Inquiry, became intrigued and desired to learn more. AI spoke to her personal identification as one who experiences life as a glass half full versus half empty and planted the seed for a year-long AI project focused on celebrating nursing at its best.

Leading this project was Karen Stefaniak, associate hospital director with the University of Kentucky Hospital/Children's Hospital and a Robert Woods Johnson Nursing Fellow. With the help of Susan Wood, an AI consultant familiar with nursing and health issues, Karen crafted *Nursing Excellence — The UK Way*. Once approved and funded for the project, Karen added Graig Casada, nurse recruiter, who brought fresh energy and enthusiasm. Together, the trio nurtured a culture of nursing appreciation that quickly spread through the entire hospital.

Their mission was simple: "AI is to become our way of life," said Karen. "I am even more convinced that AI is the way to lead and be led. The energy that has come out of our groups [AI workshops] has been unbelievable."

In December of 2003, Susan, Graig and Karen attended a weeklong AI training in Taos, NM, led by the Corporation for Positive Change — an organization dedicated to the design and development of appreciative organizations. In just four days they drafted a comprehensive plan for immediate implementation. Invigorated and with plan in hand, Karen and Graig returned to Kentucky and quickly composed a Core Team and AI partners made up of nurses and a few stakeholders to conduct a series of workshops to immediately reach 230-plus nurses, with a goal of reaching 600 or more in the future.

Armed with enthusiasm and a sense of humor, the teams chose the following topics as focus areas in the AI workshops:

- Art of Nursing
- The UK Quilt of Teamwork
- UK Magnetic Nursing
- Celebrate Life as UK Nurses
- Humor-a Vital Sign of Life

Signs of healthy nursing quickly became visible in active workshop participation and incredible storytelling. Graig shared another sign UK was realizing nursing excellence: "Seeing a few 'skeptics' at the beginning of the workshop transform into true believers by the end of the workshops. They really get it — [and experience] an 'Ah-ha!' moment. They become engaged, creative and often tell tremendous stories."

Besides creating a culture of appreciation, the projected outcome measures include nurse retention, nurse recruitment, nurse satisfaction, manager satisfaction and, depending on the measurement tool, patient satisfaction. They have compiled base line data on all outcomes that will be measured against data slated to be gathered in January of 2005.

But what can already be measured is the deep belief in their work and an improved atmosphere throughout the UK nursing community. In nearly every workshop given, nurses made 180 degree turns from feeling "negative" to recalling touching stories of their own excellence. One such story involved a nurse who walked into the workshop feeling disgruntled and out of touch. Before long, she had reconnected with her positive core values and recalled that as a young nurse she had tucked thank-you notes from patients in a special drawer at home. She left the workshop refreshed, happy and grateful for the memory, eager to spend the night revisiting her long-forgotten notes.

Equally important, several people have already asked the Core Team how the entire hospital can get involved — further signaling that a dramatic shift towards positive thinking is underway.

Vision Chicago: Sustaining Appreciative Inquiry

One large nonprofit organization utilizing Appreciative Inquiry is

World Vision, a private, volunteer organization operating relief and development efforts that impact 85 million people in nearly 100 countries. Its mission is to bring relief to areas experiencing intense suffering from war, famine, genocide and natural disasters and to develop a community's capacity to establish sustainable agriculture, viable health and education services and financial self-sufficiency. Embracing the power of positive inquiry, World Vision used it both internally as it expanded services and externally in its geographic outreach work.

Vision Chicago, part of World Vision's expanded effort to bring its expertise to U.S. cities, championed the goal of helping the city of Chicago establish large collaborative partnerships addressing difficult urban issues such as housing, education, employment and violence. Success in these environments required collaboration across dividing lines of culture, religion, geography and economic status. Over a nine-year span, Vision Chicago, mobilized a network of more than 1,500 organizations resulting in more than $6 million in direct aid, $13 million in donated products and 12,000 volunteers to invest in the health and development of the City of Chicago. Very early on, Vision Chicago became a significant success story that World Vision began replicating in other U.S. cities.

Appreciative Inquiry played an important role in Vision Chicago's plan and implementation. Mike Mantel and Jim Ludema worked together as consultants for Vision Chicago, leading the process and studying the outcomes. They used all levels of AI intervention — everything from a series of global summits to small group processes. Witnessing the power of Appreciative Inquiry in unifying people around a common direction for the future excited Mike and Jim. The process was potent: it brought together people who were rich and poor, black and white, northerners and southerners, close to home and far away to discover one another's strengths and to find agreement for collective action.

Yet, a few years after launching the initial Appreciative Inquiry process, it hit stumbling blocks; the organizational vision determined by the initial AI processes became difficult to sustain. Relational stress and staff fatigue infected the organization. At times it seemed as

13

if the progress stopped and even began regressing. Among different parties involved, words such as "war" and "camps" began to replace "invitation" and "hospitality." Exclusion competed with inclusion. What was wrong began to get more attention than what was right. Before long, critics were saying that while Appreciative Inquiry was a potent force to help people find common ground and envision a shared future, it did not sustain forward movement.

People at World Vision and Vision Chicago confronted — and tackled — a critical question: Nothing they had ever experienced could move a complex organization forward like Appreciative Inquiry, but could it stay the course — be sustained?

The answer was, resoundingly, YES! Conversations appeared to be the solution — continuous conversations. Mike and Jim discovered appreciative change was sustained by intentionally continuing positive conversational streams through inquiry at individual and corporate levels. They learned that change for Vision Chicago could be continuous, evolving, incremental and gratifying, but only by continually initiating intentional positive conversations and practicing enduring appreciative leadership.

Vision Chicago discovered that from a structural vantage point, using positive questions and an AI approach needs to be part of continuous cycles of implementation, both formally and informally, internally and externally. Regular inquiries informed and inspired new participants in the dialogue and re-inspired the old participants, spinning off fresh creativity while sustaining the positive intent needed for continued progress and success.

     *   *   *   *   *   *   *   *

As these stories demonstrate, Appreciative Inquiry (AI) highlights the identification of strengths and successes of people and organizations to plan for the future and embrace changes that inevitably occur, tapping the potential for growth. As a foundation for its work, AI uses positive questions to guide its path towards visioning, planning, redirecting, expanding and energizing an organization's work. Positive questions are affirmative. They provide the opportunity to share both personal and global experiences. By invigorating people's creative and emotional resources, positive questions open the door to breakthrough thinking.

Regardless of the setting, from small group meetings to mega, all-inclusive stakeholder "summits," positive questions and their responses produce the frame for thoughtful, creative changes utilizing past successes to build a solid future. They contribute to developing an inspiring and energetic work environment — a milieu that gathers input from all stakeholders, respects and nurtures ideas and builds on individual and collective strengths and accomplishments.

A model of organization design based on "Networks of Conversation" is emerging. More than a decade of Appreciative Inquiry experiences demonstrate communication and language are creative acts driving organizational success. With its use of positive questions, AI provides structure for engaging people in those conversations. Words are the heart of what becomes possible and provide direction and context for future success. Continuous initiation of positive conversations provides the avenue that sustains forward movement. *(See Appendix A for more information on the relationship of "networks of conversation" within the organization design field.)*

At the beginning of the 21st century, the challenges facing the non-profit sector, such as shrinking government dollars and shifting foundation priorities, have never been greater, nor have the opportunities to make a positive difference in the world. This book provides a multitude of positive questions aimed at stimulating your organization — the people you serve, your employees, volunteers and donors — to move with assurance into a clearly imagined and inviting future, generated from a positive core of strengths and values.

The opportunities revealed and energies released by the simple act of asking positive questions will amaze you!

Positive Questions and an Appreciative Inquiry
Approach for Nonprofits

This book provides valuable tools for a variety of nonprofits:

- Start-ups seeking to set a course for commitment and success
- Established organizations desiring to overcome obstacles or seeking to grow and develop in new ways
- Organizations seeking ideas for sustaining or enhancing day-to-day operations

Does your nonprofit organization:
- Seek to move in new directions?
- Occasionally stumble?
- Lack consistently high staff commitment and high morale?
- Need a boost of energy?
- Need a major overhaul?

If you answered yes to any of these questions, Read on!

The authors designed this book to enhance the performance of non-profit organizations by providing sample questions to be used in every phase of a nonprofit's organizational life. By engaging in activities that tap people's commitment to learn and serve, nonprofits can accomplish transformations with enthusiasm, ease and surprising speed.

Nonprofits are organizations that serve the public interest. Legally, they are entities organized and operated for a particular religious, charitable, educational, literary, or scientific purpose. Examples include schools, social-service agencies, volunteer service organizations, charities, various advocacy and research groups, hospitals and museums. Instead of being motivated by a quest for profit, nonprofits are organized around philosophies, beliefs, values and purposes that draw people together to achieve common goals related to the community they serve. They not only address the needs of society and culture but also the needs of individuals for inspiration, community and meaningful participation with others to make a difference in the world.

Nonprofits confront challenging times. Economic conditions prompt a growing demand for services, while fewer donors and dollars are available to meet the demand. Challenges, however, may be ripe with untapped opportunities for growth and expansion. Looking at just one sector of nonprofit activity — social services — government funding, foundation spending and private contributions have not kept pace with the needs of the poor, unemployed, uninsured and undereducated. Balancing budgets, recruiting and retaining staff and maintaining a high level of service pose unprecedented challenges for board and staff members, committed donors, contractors and volunteers. In many communities, untapped opportunities led to increased collaboration among agencies, expanding resources and extending services in spite of the new challenges.

When using or adapting the questions, nonprofits should focus on the life-giving aspects of their organization: the purposes for which they were formed and the ends to which they are working — that which imbues their efforts with excitement and energy.

Most nonprofits evaluate themselves periodically and embark on changes in response to evolving needs. Transformation begins with the simple act of people talking about their passions and core interests. Positive questions promote change and growth by uncovering incredible untapped energy unlocked by storytelling about successful experiences that can form the foundation for expanded positive futures.

The Power of Positive Questions

The wise man doesn't give the right answers, he poses the right questions.

—Claude Levi-Strauss

The AI process builds upon the "positive psychology" movement that took shape with Dr. Martin Seligman during his term as president of the American Psychological Association in 1998. Dr. Seligman asserted that "Psychology is not just the study of weaknesses and damage, it is also the study of strength and virtue. Treatment is not just fixing what is broken; it is nurturing what is best within ourselves." His inquiry into 30 years of psychological research yielded 45,000 studies of depression and only 300 of joy. Dr. Seligman challenged his colleagues to embrace positive psychology. Appreciative Inquiry, with its emphasis on the use of affirmative questions, uses the concepts behind "positive psychology" to amplify strengths as a way to repair or overcome weaknesses.

Words Create Worlds...Positive Images Produce Positive Actions

Why ask positive questions? People and organizations live in the worlds their words create. Negative questions, such as "Why do we have such low morale?" or "Why can't people work out their differences?" focus our attention on all the things that are wrong. By shifting that focus towards the positive, "What are the best things about working here?" or "What can we do together to build on the strength of our relationship?" we find solutions rather than more problems and blame. Asking and answering positive questions generates new ideas, enthusiasm and commitment among staff, boards of directors, volunteers, service recipients and community members working with nonprofit organizations.

The use of positive questions, whether as a foundation for a structured Appreciative Inquiry or as a means to enhance communication, understanding and commitment within a group, leads us down many paths with potential for growth and change. Positive questions encourage people to share peak experiences, values, hopes and dreams and elicit stories and aspirations that generate connections. The act of asking and answering positive questions generates constructive thinking and actions and offers direction to further dialogue and planning. Positive, affirmative questions mobilize people's minds and hearts in service of an organization's vision, mission, values and goals. Nonprofits can tap this potential leading to a vibrant and successful future.

Writing positive questions is more art than science. To be effective, questions must be clear, compelling and provocative. The authors of The Power of Appreciative Inquiry: A Practical Guide to Positive Change polled interviewers to determine what makes positive questions effective. The following were some of the interviewers' suggestions. Positive questions:

- *Help to forge personal connections between interviewers and interviewees.* They have a conversational quality to them and convey unconditional positive regard.
- *Invite stories, rather than abstract opinions or theories.* They're introduced by phrases like "Tell me about" and "Describe to me."
- *Are personal, almost intimate.* They ask people to describe something with which they strongly identify and/or remember something or someone that matters.
- *Draw on people's life and work experience.* They give people a chance to learn and draw meaning from episodes and experiences that might otherwise have escaped their attention.
- *Invoke a mental scan.* They force people to think about powerfully positive experiences or insights and to choose the best of the best.
- *Are sometimes ambiguous.* They give people room to swim around, to answer in a variety of ways.
- *Walk people through an inner journey.* They ask people to interpret or deconstruct what worked or was meaningful about things that they may have taken for granted.
- *Are uplifting.* They paint positive and attractive pictures inspiring people to consider new possibilities.

- *Give free rein to the imagination.* They take people into possible futures and help them imagine positive possibilities.
- *Suggest action.* They help people consider immediate next steps.
- *Have an emotional and logical flow to them.* As the interview moves from one question to the next, people are inspired and enlivened to find deeper meaning

---

If you truly wish to change your world, you must change your way of asking questions. It could be that the moment you do so a totally different world will take shape around you.

Encyclopedia of Positive Questions—Volume One

What constitutes a positive (appreciative) approach for an interview?

- **The title of an affirmative topic.** This is a short, positive phrase that describes a desired outcome, behavior, or goal. Affirmative topics set the stage for envisioning and enacting the future by reflecting the desired direction of your organization. In short, they set the agenda.

    One example is:
    Walking Confidently in the Direction of Our Dreams

- **A lead-in statement.** This introduces an affirmative topic and describes it as already existing. It provides a context for people's experiences and insights inspiring enthusiasm for the topic.

    The lead-in statement for our affirmative topic example is:

    All nonprofits exist with purpose: they focus on serving an unmet need or future dream for a chosen community or client group. A sense of purpose can be a dream, a vision or both, but most effectively includes input from all parties impacted by the organization. A vibrant and clear vision illuminates a collective direction, full of purpose and

meaning: a foundation for moving an organization inten-
tionally and confidently forward.

1. ***A series of positive questions.*** The questions have a past,
   present and future orientation. Effective questions are
   generally structured around the four phases of AI:
   Discovery is generally a "best of what is" question.
   Dream taps into the visions people hold related to the topic.
   Design probes what the person has to say about the topic and
   begins to uncover how the ideal situation might be created.
   Destiny envisions the future regarding the topic.

Oftentimes an interviewer combines these ideas depending on the
topic and the setting.

In an Appreciative Inquiry or similar group process, interviews with
positive questions are the keystone for positive inquiries leading to
transformation of people and their organizations. High-quality
questions invite respondents to explore a topic emotionally,
intellectually and sensually. Interviewers are not just interested in
collecting data and facts. They want to hear about the whole range of
people's experiences.

Guide to an Engaging Interview Process

Here are helpful suggestions for conducting powerful interviews leading to change.

1. Determine the topic to be addressed.

2. Use or modify this book's topic titles, lead-ins and questions to meet the needs of the organization. Note that two important points are to keep everything positive and to look to an ideal future.

3. Have copies of the questions available for each participant. Putting space between the printed questions for taking notes allows the interviewer to capture important points that will be shared later. Distribute the questions, after the process has been explained. This gives participants a few minutes to read and think about the questions and their responses and they can give their full attention to the interview process when it begins.

4. Plan the interview approach in advance. Two possible strategies are:

   • Interpersonal Interviews. Two people interview each other for a predetermined amount of time for each person to be interviewed. The interviews work best if people pair up with someone they don't know well because cross-department or cross job partners can generate especially rich ideas. Use numbering off, a self-selection honor system, or have pre-assignments to determine pairs. Determine an objective way to decide who will be the first interviewer. One method is to ask the partners to determine who has the next closest birthday.

   • Interview team. A team of interviewers is selected and trained on how to conduct the interviews. A designated team of people disperse throughout an organization with each team member interviewing multiple people using a pre-determined set of questions. A diverse sample, for both the interview team and the interviewee's is critical. The more diversity, including a cross-section of job positions, the richer the conversations will be.

22

5. Before the interviews begin, the facilitator or discussion leader explains the concepts of using positive questions and seeking success stories as the basis for future growth. For example, "We will be emphasizing the key attributes of Appreciative Inquiry that help us look at...
   - Discovering the best of our past and present.
   - Dreaming about what might be.
   - Designing what we want to be.
   - Creating our destiny — our ideal future — with ideas to achieve it."
   - Emphasize that all information is valuable and will be integrated into the planning progress.

6. Interview rules:
   - One person has a specified amount of time to interview another person —from 15 minutes to more than an hour. The time allotted is dependent on the depth of the material and questions.

   - Because the group will later share some of their insights, encourage the interviewer to jot down some <u>key</u> points on the interview sheet.

   - This is an exercise in intentional listening by the interviewer. The interviewer does not step in and take over, no matter how tempting it might be to add his/her personal and related stories.

   - By using verbal and non-verbal cues, the interviewer encourages thoughtful and in-depth responses. Expanding on the printed questions with additional open-ended and probing queries helps the interviewees' ideas to fully blossom.

   - Even if the written set of questions is completed before the ending time, the interviewer continues to ask additional positive questions to help "stretch" the inquiry and elicit more story details, feelings and ideas for the future.

   - The facilitator should give a verbal warning about 3/4 of the way through the allotted time, giving everyone a chance to complete the questions.

- Encourage creativity and openness. The interview process should be fun!

7. Capture the essence. As the interviews progress, the facilitator should listen and watch for behaviors such as body language, energy levels and intensity of the conversations that give clues to the participants' engagement. Later, the facilitator will share the observations.

Soliciting main themes and ideas from the process is crucial. Participants feel they have engaged in a worthwhile process when their ideas are captured and recorded. Several of the stories in this book give examples of how the ideas were summarized and disseminated. Sharing highlights from each question and recording them on flipchart pages is one standard method for capturing information. Facilitator manuals have many other creative ways to capture the information. If desired, the information can be further synthesized into main themes or ideas, either through a voting process or small group to synthesize the information.

Whatever methods you use to capture the essence of the interviewees' positive responses, sharing that information with everyone in your organization is constructive and appreciated. Related projects, or other ways to continue conversations, can also be built into this process. For example, if the theme of the inquiry is creating a more satisfying work environment, each team can commit to using its data to develop ways to foster satisfaction and enjoyment in the workplace. Each team's project can also be shared with all! Other possible methods to share include newsletters, posters, memos, formal reports or a simple email alert.

Pay attention to the questions you need to ask, not the answers you want to hear.

—Leonard Hirsch

Many compelling questions in this book provide nonprofits the opportunity to tap into their energy, passion and strengths to drive an organization forward with surprising speed and clarity of purpose. Within the book, three main sections focus on the operation of your nonprofit.
- The Big Picture
- The People
- The Infrastructure

The Big Picture: Being Successful

Effective organizational design structures and systems are key to the overall functioning of your organization. Whether you are a start-up, developing, or well-established organization, your success depends on your ability to lead and manage. The board of directors has the duty of setting a direction and overseeing the accomplishment of the goals in a legally and financially responsible way.

The community also plays an integral role in the success of your nonprofit. Given the continuous need for and perennial shortfalls of, financial revenue, it may be imperative that the community works together to stretch limited resources. Nonprofits can achieve long-term, meaningful and sustainable results through cooperation among the board, administration, management and the community.

Questions in this section focus on:

- Vision, Mission, Values and Outcomes
- Governance
- Leadership
- Planning
- Financial Sustainability, Marketing and Public Relations
- Partnerships, Collaborations and the Community

The People: Considering Everyone Important
to Your Organization

People are your greatest asset and greatest resource. They are the core and fiber of what you do. Staff, volunteers, donors and service recipients thrive in an organization that exudes an atmosphere of appreciation and respect. Effectively utilizing each person's talents and passions, nonprofits expand scarce resources while bringing joy to those involved. Actively engaging people in all aspects of the organization assures a strong and healthy corporation.

These questions address recruitment, selection, retention, training, recognition and satisfaction of all the people within your organization:

- Donors
- Volunteers
- Service Recipients
- Staff
- Management

The Infrastructure: Operating Efficiently and Effectively
Day-to-Day

The infrastructure is the backbone of an organization — when healthy, it promotes strength and vitality. The tangible and intangible aspects of the infrastructure support everything that occurs within the organization, from day-to-day communications to the tools that track and manage short and long-term aspects of the nonprofit. Care and attention to the infrastructure, demonstrated by input and involvement from those within the organization, assures a stable, firm foundation for your nonprofit.

The questions concentrate on:

- Culture and Climate of the Workplace
- Financial Systems
- Managing and Using Data and Technology
- Time Management

26

Our questions provide opportunities for conversations throughout a nonprofit and its community to enhance relationships and effectiveness, as well as guidance in framing an Appreciative Inquiry process. While this book assumes some knowledge of Appreciative Inquiry, it is not intended for the exclusive use of those who are trained in, or have experience with, AI techniques. You will find a multitude of questions in this section, on numerous topics. *(See Appendix B for a brief overview of the Appreciative Inquiry Process.)* Of course, you may want to modify some of them to apply precisely to your organization's situation and purposes. Some questions are written in first person, some in third person. How the interviews are conducted and with whom will determine which "voice" is appropriate for your situation. We invite you to try them out and to adapt them to the needs of your organization.

The questions are designed for a nonprofit to pick and choose according to the situation, issues and needs the organization faces. Few organizations would use all these questions or approach them in the chronological order as presented.

The most effective way of using these topics is to determine the situation or setting where they will be applied and adapt your selection accordingly. For example, the topic *Meetings Matter*, located under the section *Big Picture* and the category of *Governance,* looks at what is important to board members for engaging, productive and successful meetings. However, the questions could easily be used as written, or adjusted slightly, for staff, since they, too, must attend designated meetings. Therefore the *Meetings Matter* questions could be used to generate ideas for what would make staff meetings or training sessions more meaningful and inspiring.

The following chart lists the three major sections, the categories within each section and individual topics within each category. Each topic has an affirmative title, a lead-in description and positive, compelling questions for use in generating identification of strengths, direction and energy.

Dig in. Have fun. Experiment. Create.

Index of Topics: 80 Positive Questions for Nonprofits.

The Big Picture — Section I

#	Vision, Mission, Values and Outcomes
1	Walking Confidently in the Direction of Our Dreams
2	Making a Difference Our Way
3	Tapping Our Heart's Desire
4	Continually Moving Forward
5	Sustaining Commitment
6	Keeping Our Eyes on the Ball
7	Realizing Results

#	Governance
8	The Right People at the Board Table
9	Engaging Board Members' Full Participation
10	Meetings Matter
11	Ideal Board and Staff Relations

#	Leadership
12	The Art of Giving Leadership Away
13	Leadership Helping All to Shine Brightly
14	Who's Running This Show Anyway?
15	Modeling Integrity
16	Inspiring a Work Climate of Confidence and Trust
17	Walk the Talk: Set the Tone
18	Tough Decisions
19	Making the Most of Change

#	Planning
20	Adapting to Trends
21	Strategic Planning
22	Uniqueness: Defining our Niche
23	Learning Across Cultures
24	Evaluating Services and Successes

The People — Section I

The Infrastructure — Section III

#	Managing and Using Data and Technology
76	Technology Extending and Enhancing Our Work
77	Better Databases for Better Performance
78	Our Numbers Define Us

#	Time Management
79	The Right Things First
80	Tick-Tock: Time Management

The Nonprofits' Guide to the Power of Appreciative inquiry

Walking Confidently in the Direction of Our Dreams

All nonprofits exist with purpose: they focus on serving an unmet need or future dream for a chosen community or client group. A sense of purpose can be a dream, a vision or both, but most effectively includes input from all parties impacted by the organization. A vibrant and clear vision illuminates a collective direction, full of purpose and meaning: a foundation for moving an organization intentionally and confidently forward.

1. What inspired you to found or join this organization? How do you describe its purpose? What does being part of this organization mean to you?

2. Tell about a time when you observed the vision of the organization being accomplished in big or small ways. What was happening? Who was involved? What part did you play?

3. What do you believe are the most important parts of the organization's vision?

    • What are the key factors that will strengthen the power of this vision in the future?
    • What part will you play in keeping the vision alive?

2.

Making a Difference Our Way

The country has nearly one million nonprofit organizations, each with a unique set of guiding principles, target population, services and expected outcomes. However, most nonprofits share a common goal — to make a difference by having a positive impact in the world.

To be extraordinary, an organization must clearly articulate its goals, boast about its achievements and bolster support for its contribution to the community it serves. "I am the greatest!" Muhammed Ali proclaimed. Sports enthusiasts debate whether he was, but he convinced himself and millions of others that he was a winner. Understanding your nonprofit's purpose and articulating this uniqueness helps ensures support from a vibrant and committed membership, staff and community.

[Prepare ahead of time]
The mission statement of this organization is:

1. Tell me about a situation where you were involved in a powerful success story with this organization. What supported this happening? Who was involved and what were their roles and actions? What important role did you play in this success story?

2. Let's talk about what makes this organization unique. What did this organization accomplish that others couldn't? What factors allowed it to create such a success?

34

3. Take a moment to think about your organization's strengths. What are they? What related strengths do you, personally, have?

4. You are in an elevator and someone enthusiastically asks, "you work here!?" Develop a 20 second description that captures your enthusiasm and commitment about the organization. This is your chance to tout its greatness! Have fun!

5. You are developing a promotional poster. What five words would most strongly convey the essence of this organization?

3.

Tapping Our Heart's Desire

A successful organization has a core passion or principle that inspires the direction and scope of its work, clarifies the organization's actions and eliminates activities that are not aligned with its goals. Thus, an organization gains tremendous power to refocus and reenergize everyone involved. Tapping into the heart's desire — or core — of the organization opens the door to realizing the big picture, making its purpose a reality and ensuring its vitality for years to come.

1. How would you describe the core passion that motivates the people of your organization and to which you are committed?

2. What is your role in accomplishing your organization's big picture?

3. What are the primary accomplishments of others toward your organization's common goals?

4. What key factors are present when people are acting in a manner most aligned with the big picture?

5. Imagine a future where everyone is focused on the organization's core passion and principles. What does it look like? How did your organization get everyone on the same page? What are the outcomes of this incredible unity?

4.

Continually Moving Forward

"All eyes ahead. Forward. March." These calls are an effective way to move a high school band down the parade route. Organizations, however, have a different set of directions. When we talk about forward movement in an organization, we mean the alignment and progression of everyone towards the direction of its vision. The route leading there is not easily defined; the way people travel the route varies. Some will be walking on the road, others running on sidewalks or cycling alternate routes; some routes will be shorter, others longer — but everyone is working to achieve the same outcomes. *When the organization's big picture motivates everyone, they make it to the finish line no matter what path they take.*

1. Tell me a story about a time you experienced being a part of a group or organization where everyone embraced a common direction — even though they made different contributions to its success. What was its goal? What role did you play? What roles did others play?

2. Now describe what supported that result. What did leadership contribute? How did you know where the organization was going? What systems, structures and communications were in place to assure a coordinated effort?

3. What do you expect of a leader who is responsible for moving an organization forward? What characteristics and qualities contribute to success? What attitudes are essential?

4. As a leader in your organization, five years from now National Public Radio is interviewing you and asks about your organization's recent progress and how it succeeded so wonderfully. What part did leadership play? What did you do that assured the whole organization moved in the direction determined by its leadership? What are five major points that you want to highlight?

5.

Sustaining Commitment

Many motivating factors drive people to work everyday. Tapping into those motivations, sustaining the commitment of that staff and providing meaningful work is an important charge for any organization. Developing guiding principles and values for the organization helps assure a common approach to the organization's work. When staff is involved in establishing those guiding principles and values, they embrace them as their own. The organization, its members, staff and recipients of service all benefit from sustained commitment and enthusiasm.

1. Describe what motivates you to get up each morning. What are the things, people or situations you would not want to miss each day?

2. How do these motivating factors reflect your personal values? How are these values reflected in your work?

3. What are the values or principles you hold so strongly that if they were not present in your work situation you would have to say, "I'm out of here!"?

4. What is your experience of sharing your principles/values with others in an organizational setting? How does that impact your commitment to the organization? What will you do to keep these principles and values alive?

6.

Keeping Our Eyes on the Ball

An organization has desired outcomes reflected in its vision, mission and values. Revisiting the vision, mission and values and involving all staff in some aspect of this process is important to make everyone feel like a meaningful part of every success. To that end, a universal focus on outcomes is key for reaching an organization's desired destination.

1. Think of a time when you were part of a team, board, organization, or special project that was clearly focused on the outcome. How did this impact the scope of the work accomplished? What was your experience in being a part of the team, board, organization or project?

2. What is the focus for your organization? How has your organization kept all eyes on outcomes? How has it helped to have this focus?

3. Imagine that over the next three years your organization accomplishes three major tasks. Now imagine it achieved these by keeping focused and, possibly, regrouping as necessary to ensure focus was maintained. What was accomplished? Who was involved? What, if any, regrouping occurred? How did this focus benefit the organization and serve its recipients?

40

7.

Realizing Results

Constantly striving for outcomes that support the organization's goals and reflect its vision inspires extraordinary results. By establishing a few specific conditions of satisfaction, an organization can more effectively move in the direction of its dreams and channel activities to ensure those outcomes are met. Examples of outcomes might include, "a clean environment," "fewer teen births," "enhanced literacy levels," "increased eagle populations," "greater access to health care," "positive political leadership" and "increased voter registration." Once clearly delineated, outcomes become the barometer for measuring the effectiveness of activities developed to achieve the outcome.

1. Think about an experience of being given an assignment where only the "outcome" was defined for you? For example: you'd been asked to arrange for a "fun family picnic." That was the expected outcome. What did you do to ensure that "desired result?" Describe the situation and the activities you planned. How did you carry them out?

2. What do you see as the desired outcomes for your nonprofit organization? How do you see the organization's systems and activities supporting achieving those outcomes?

3. What do you see as the "outcome(s)" of your particular work or position as it relates to the organization? How will you help your department/unit in achieving the organization's outcomes? What can you do to direct your activities toward the organization's outcomes?

41

8.

The Right People at the Board Table

A nonprofit board of directors relies on the voluntary participation of people who believe in its services, mission and goals. The "dream board" for most nonprofits consists of members who represent potential partner organizations in the community, are influential, have needed skills and provide invaluable guidance and support.

Board nominating committees, driven to create dynamic boards reflective of the community served, generally have the responsibility to recruit and recommend new board members. Seeking the input of the full board, the staff and well-positioned community leaders provides the foundation for choosing the right people for the job.

1. Tell me about a particularly positive experience you had serving on a nonprofit board of directors. What was your role on the board? What was it about the service on the board that made it fulfilling and positive?

2. This organization is casting a net far and wide to identify people who represent our community as possible board members. What is the first thing that comes to your mind when I ask, "What kind of person would be good for this board?" What skills, knowledge, expertise, stature in the community, etc., do you envision this person possessing?

3. What will you contribute to the nominating committee in securing new board members?

4. Imagine that it is this time next year. Your organization has an energetic and involved board made up of the kinds of people you and others have suggested. What makes this board the dream board of this organization's future?

9.

Engaging Board Members' Full Participation

At some point in their history, most nonprofit organizations face a challenge in sustaining consistent board member attendance and active engagement with the organization. Board members are frequently selected because of their community status, fund raising potential and expertise, or to increase the scope of community representation on the board. Selecting board members is as important as offering them an enriching board member experience. Successful boards (and board members) are those that continue to expand themselves individually and collectively, bringing fresh perspectives as well as wisdom to the organization.

1. Think about a time when you and other board members felt most engaged and committed to supporting the organization. What was happening? Who was involved? Did anyone outside the board participate in a meaningful way to achieving success? What role did you play in making the board successful?

2. Describe the values, core competencies and behaviors present in a truly engaged board.

3. How do you know when board members are actively participating and enthusiastically engaged in the work of the board?

4. Tell me about the skills and talents of your board members. How could they be more effectively tapped?

5. Imagine it's a year from now. The entire board of directors has been present for every meeting over the last six months, arriving early, ready to participate, making contributions to the discussion and actively involved in subcommittee work. Your board has decided to expand its membership and you have eagerly volunteered to write an announcement soliciting prospective board members. What would the announcement say?

10.

Meetings Matter

"Roll call — all present" are sweet words to a board chairperson, board member and executive director's ears. Making meetings matter is an important step to good attendance. When all members are present, business proceeds in a timely manner. Healthy board attendance signals that members feel mutual respect and a commitment to a shared vision and that their precious personal time is well used. Making meetings efficient and effective encourages commitment. Members who feel that their time is well spent will attend regularly.

1. Describe some meetings you have experienced as being well run and effective. What were some elements that really stood out? How was an effective meeting organized? What materials were available? How did each person interact? How did you feel about the use of your time?

2. How can we make meetings more meaningful and productive? What makes you want to attend?

3. A year from now your board attendance has risen dramatically and more work is completed in a timely manner. Prepare your main points for a newsletter article describing the changes that contributed to the increased commitment and attendance. How did these things happen and who was responsible for their implementation? What are some quotes you might include from members?

Ideal Board and Staff Relations

In a successful organization a winning alliance exists among the board, the CEO and staff that promotes efficient systems and services. The board is involved in the program but does not micromanage. Board members are informed, support program staff and provide guidance and oversight. The CEO and staff carry out the work. Together, they are aligned to achieve the organization's goals and mission. A positive and mutually supportive relationship among board members, staff and the CEO carries the organization in the direction of its dreams.

This relationship is like a musical production. Boards "select the music" and "play" the supporting bass parts, the CEO "conducts" the ensemble, while staff "play the melody." Hitting different notes and playing different instruments, boards and staff eventually harmonize to "play the same tune." Through this harmony their work becomes nearly seamless and positively benefits the community they serve.

1. Tell me about your best experience with boards and staff "playing the same tune." Using the music analogy, what were the "notes" each group played? What made it all work together? What did you contribute to making it a notable experience?

2. Describe the type of "music" you hear coming from your organization. What part does the board play in your current organization? What parts do the CEO and staff play?

3. Describe the type of music you would like to hear coming from your organization. What are the things you are doing or will do to contribute to this music? How can you help in creating "harmony" and "resolving dissonance?"

4. Imagine it is a year from now and your organization has an even more successful board/program staff relationship. Describe what has changed and how change was implemented.

12.

The Art of Giving Leadership Away

In the last 25 years, more organizations — both profit and nonprofit — realized their viability depends on innovation, flexibility and agility to adjust to society's ever-changing needs. The "official" leadership in today's successful organizations engages people at all levels to care about, contribute to and celebrate in the organization's achievements, that is to become "unofficial" leaders. Today's enterprises flourish by developing leaders throughout their organization: tapping the contributions of all their available human resources.

In the Taoist tradition, an "official" leader creates leadership among others through invisible empowerment actions to achieve greatness and expand the overall capacity of the entire organization.

> *Of a good leader,*
> *When his task is done,*
> *His work complete,*
> *The people say...*
> *We did this ourselves.*
>
> Lao Tzu from the Tao de Ching 6th century B.C.

1. Think about a time in an organization when leadership was visible at all levels — it may have been in isolated instances or unplanned, but it was present nonetheless. Who was involved? What was happening? What results were produced? What was your contribution?

2. What was the "official" leadership doing or saying? What values were communicated about the work and how to get it done?

3. How could the development of leaders, at all levels of your organization, be more fully expanded? What capacities need to be further developed? What training is needed? What risks need to be taken? What accountability structures need to be developed?

4. Envision what the organization's leadership looks like three years from now. Describe a conversation between "official" leaders and others in the organization before, during and after accomplishing a particularly successful task of vital importance to the organization.

13.

Leadership Helping All to Shine Brightly

Daniel Goleman's extremely popular book, <u>Primal Leadership</u>, promotes the concept that leaders set the tone for their organizations. "If a leader radiates energy and enthusiasm, an organization thrives; if a leader spreads negativity and dissonance, it flounders," Goleman pens. Leadership, sparked by vision, passion and purpose, can ignite an organization and send it blazing toward its destiny. In the glow of such leadership, others find fulfillment and satisfaction and discover their own brightness. As a result, the organization shines and basks in its myriad accomplishments.

1. Describe a leader who sparked an organization to great achievements. How did he/she ignite the organization? How did others respond to this glowing leadership?

2. Where does leadership shine brightly in your organization? How would you describe the elements of that leadership? How do your actions reflect that leadership?

3. Envision your organization three years into the future. All employees are "ablaze" with energy, ideas and commitment to the organization largely because of what the leadership has done. What made this fusion of energy, ideas and commitment possible? Describe changes that have been made — new systems, policies, practices, motivations and expectations. How do you feel about your leaders?

14.

Who's Running this Show Anyway?

In the best organizations leadership exists at all levels — every person who inspires others is a leader. Adopting this leadership perspective has great potential for calling forth the best throughout the organization. Organizations with leaders who empower others and are advocates for positive energy forge ahead to make extraordinary differences in the institutions and communities they serve.

1. Tell me how leaders in your organization invite others in non-leadership positions to contribute as leaders. When have you felt like a leader? How did that feel? What did it inspire you to do in other areas of your work?

2. What would your organization look like if everyone was encouraged to take on leadership roles from time to time? Describe the experience of working in such an organization.

3. What would it take for your organization to become an even more successful place because leadership exists at all levels? What could your organization accomplish as a result of empowering leadership throughout the whole organization?

Modeling Integrity

Integrity is being what you stand for. Organizations that model alignment with their values demonstrate integrity. Leadership that exemplifies integrity enthusiastically supports all members of an organization to "live and be" models of the core mission and values.

1. Remember a time in your agency, when someone demonstrated integrity. What was the situation? Who was there? What developed? How did it feel to you and others involved?

2. What are the agency values demonstrated in the story you shared? What do these values mean to you on a personal level?

3. What if everyday, 100% of the time, 100% of the employees modeled these values? What would it look like? What would your agency be doing? How would your daily energy be focused?

16.

Inspiring a Work Climate of Confidence and Trust

We all have people in whom we have absolute confidence and trust: a spouse, a friend, a parent or relative. Organizations with people in leadership roles who evoke that same kind of confidence and trust are fortunate. Such leaders inspire their employees and people they serve. When people feel trusted and confident, the doors of limitless possibilities open!

1. Think about a time when you had the utmost confidence and trust in a leader. What experiences evoked those feelings of trust? How did you know that you had absolute trust in the leader?

2. Describe a time when a leader showed trust and confidence in you. What was the situation? How did you know you were trusted? What actions did it inspire you to take? What were the results?

3. Describe a time when you were in a leadership position (either at work or elsewhere) where you felt that you inspired trust in those you led. What did you do to earn that?

4. Two years from now you are asked to write a newsletter article on the ways in which leaders inspire trust from the staff. What points will you emphasize?

17.

Walk the Talk: Set the Tone

The world and workplaces shine when leaders lead by example. The leader whose walk and talk are congruent inspires and attracts a dedicated following. Leadership is responsible for setting the tone and demonstrating, on a daily basis, what the organization is about. Effectively "walking the talk" calls for internal and external self-reflection and commitment. "Walking the talk" successfully inspires others to believe in the organization's core values and encourages others to follow the leader's model of integrity.

1. Describe a leader who has "walked the talk." Tell me about a situation where this was visible. What were the behaviors that you noticed? How did you know that his/her actions were consistent with his/her talk? How did you respond?

3. Tell me a story about a time you acted in a manner truly "in tune" with your core beliefs — when you "walked the talk." What were the circumstances? What were the outcomes? How did others around you respond?

3. You are writing a book on "walking the talk" in your organization. Tell me ideas you would include in the following chapters:

    • Behaviors that reflect our vision, mission and values.

    • How we demonstrate who we are as an organization and what we do.

    • How we support each other in "walking our talk."

18.

Tough Decisions

Taking the risk of making a decision is a defining characteristic of leadership. As Harry S. Truman so famously stated, "The Buck Stops Here." Decisions are evaluated against their ability to fulfill an organization's mission, vision and values. Making decisions is easy when everyone supports you, but challenges often arise in the face of new ideas. A successful leader makes decisions that will lead the organization to increased success — even in the face of organizational resistance to change.

1. Tell me about a time you made a decision that had an important impact on your life or organization — a decision where others were not supportive. What went into making this choice? What alternatives did you consider? How did you define success in this situation?

2. Tell me how you approach making difficult decisions. What factors do you consider? From whom do you seek input? How do you respond to their input? What steps do you take to attract others regardless of their support for your decision?

3. Based on your experiences with challenging decision-making, what are three or more key lessons you would share with others in a similar situation?

Making the Most of Change

Like the wind, change can be refreshing. It breezes through things clearing the air and opening new opportunities. An inevitable part of all of life and every organization, change can awaken exploration of new beginnings and unlock dynamic energy. With change comes the opportunity for growth that can move individuals and organizations into new and exciting possibilities.

1. Describe a time when you were confronted by change. What did you do to successfully change? What resources did you use through the time of change? How did you benefit or create opportunities as a result of the change?

2. What do you value about yourself when you are dealing with change?

3. List three wishes for others in your organization to enhance their ability to embrace change.

4. What suggestions would you make for your organization to make effective changes — changes that may be necessary for its continued success?

20.

Adapting to Trends

Organizations stay viable by proactively responding to current trends and emerging needs. Adaptive organizations take the initiative to respond to new ideas or outside forces. Four qualities seem to define this ability: having an external focus, utilizing networking connections, encouraging inquisitiveness and being innovative. Viewing changing trends as opportunities for expanded service ensures organizational growth and fosters rewarding experiences.

1. Share a story that illustrates how you responded in a positive manner to a need or new trend in any situation. What was the need or trend? What were your reactions? What did you do? Who did you involve? How did others respond?

2. Using an external focus, what are the trends you currently see that relate to the mission of this organization? What are the opportunities for expanded or redirected service? With what other entities should your organization be connected to respond to these trends?

3. What motivates you to respond with positive emotions and actions to changes and new ideas? What support do you need to be adaptive?

4. A year from now this organization is being recognized by the state Governor with the "Staying Current - Seizing Opportunities" award. You have been asked to write some bullet points for the Governor's award speech. What points

would help others understand how your organization seized the opportunity to respond to current community trends and needs?

21.

Strategic Planning

A strategic plan is a tool to help your organization plan for the future. The process of strategic planning produces decisions shaping and guiding an organization's future. Board members and staff collaborate to develop a roadmap featuring opportunities and challenges to match the organization's strengths, needs for growth and adaptation to shifting trends beyond its immediate span of influence. In addition to providing a guiding document for the agency, more funders require a strategic plan illustrating where they might fit into your priorities. This intensive planning project takes time and a commitment — time well spent preparing an organization for its best future.

1. Tell me about a time when you planned, far in advance, for a major event or investment. How far into the future were you planning? What was the impact? Describe the steps you took and who helped you.

2. Pretend your organization is undertaking a strategic planning process:

    -   Besides the board and staff, name some outside stakeholders you might tap for input.
    -   What current program strengths will the plan identify?
    -   What are some current trends that will impact the organization?
    -   What might the impacts be?
    -   What possible new directions do you see emerging from the future trends?

3. You are holding your organization's new beautifully bound strategic plan. Unfortunately, the fate of some strategic plans is to collect dust on a shelf. What must happen next that ensures it is used? What is the responsibility of the board, CEO and staff? How might you contribute to its implementation?

22.

Uniqueness: Defining our Niche

Each nonprofit should fill a unique niche in society. Outsiders or potential donors want assurances that services are not replicating others and that scarce community resources are being effectively utilized. A mission statement gives a broad picture of who you are, but your programs and activities more clearly define your role within the community.

A vital, successful organization assures that everyone affiliated with it can describe its unique identity with clarity. Similarly, effective public relations efforts must support and highlight an organization's distinctive qualities.

1. As you think about this organization, what questions do friends and acquaintances ask you about it services? How do you answer them? What words and phrases do you find yourself using over and over again in your description?

2. What do you see are the unique values and principles that this organization has internalized into its overall philosophy and everyday practices? Which of your personal values is met through your involvement with this organization?

3. When you talk to satisfied users of this service, what are they saying? Why are they members or clients?

4. Imagine you are developing a marketing advertisement and you have to develop five phrases or words that describe the uniqueness of this organization — why it is different from other similar services? Tell me about the words or phrases and why you chose them?

23.

Learning Across Cultures

Successful nonprofits strive to learn from each other within a diverse workplace. When all voices – including age, ethnicity, gender, race, religion, political-leanings, sexual preference, abilities and income levels – are represented and inter-cultural communication is strong, people will learn from each other. Organizations recognizing and building upon the strengths of everyone are closer to realizing their goals, dreams and visions. Listening to and incorporating ideas from everyone, expands the possibilities for greatness.

1. Tell me about a time when you observed extraordinary communication between cultures, either within an organization or in your personal experiences. Describe the benefits and learnings for each person.

2. What do you value about the way members of diverse backgrounds work together within your organization? Give specific examples of ways your organization's culture illustrates the ideal model of learning from one another.

3. Imagine your organization ten years from now. The population the organization serves has changed dramatically in terms of diversity and culture. You are assuring funders and donors that the organization consistently adapts to changes and that its good works continue. Make a list of five "talking points" for how "learning across cultures" has been fostered. What are the results you see and feel?

24.

Evaluating Services and Successes

Knowing when an organization has performed well is rewarding and reinforcing. Determining an outcome and then measuring for success creates a road map for the organization's actions as well as a system for accountability. An oft-asked question is, "If you don't know where you are going, how will you know if you got there?" By establishing milestones and measuring steps along the way, an organization continually evaluates its progress. Identifying, recognizing and celebrating successes reinforces the organization's work and inspires everyone to continue paving the path to future success.

1. Tell me about a time you planned for an event or activity that went really well. How did you know it went well? How did the success leave you and others feeling?

2. How do you know when you have made a positive contribution to a work event or task or activity?

3. Be boastful as you tell me how you can contribute to this organization and its successes. How will you inspire others to do the same?

4. What will keep you inspired and committed to this organization's successes and having measurable results?

5. In five years you are searching the internet and you "Google" this organization's name; you find more than 100 entries listed and note that one is about its overwhelming success in reaching a lofty goal. What does the article share about this organization's work over the past five years?
    Who was involved? How was work monitored?
    How was achievement determined? Rewarded?

Stewardship of Funds

The board of directors in a nonprofit organization has legal and fiscal responsibilities for the organization. Boards set financial policies and monitor its financial status on an ongoing basis. These responsibilities necessitate that boards approve the annual budget, monitor the budget against actual fiscal performance, oversee the audit, check management of investments where appropriate and comply with tax and other laws as well as funders' regulations. Carrying this out entails an understanding of the required fiscal reporting and how it is executed. The CEO makes the day-to-day spending decisions within the board's plan and oversees the use of resources.

Well-functioning boards ask these questions: *Are we on target with expenses and revenues? Are we financially solvent? Will we have income for our future expenses?* Only a continuous interplay among the board, CEO and employees leads to an effective stewardship of funds and resources.

1. Think back to a time when you or someone else in the organization clearly contributed to its fiscal well-being. What were some of the thoughts you had about the organization's finances and your responsibility? What did you do? What did others do?

2. Within your current organization, what do you see as your responsibility related to the organization's resources? Even if you never handle money, what do you consider your responsibility related to the organization's funds?

3. What are the values or principles that you consider essential for all staff related to the organization's resources? How would you promote these values/principles?

4. Imagine you are at your organization's annual dinner. A guest asks you to describe how your organization provided accurate oversight of public and private funds this past year. What could you tell him or her about the stewardship of funds? How do you know? What additional information would you need to feel confident in what you were saying?

26.

Applying for Grants

Securing grant money is a necessity for nonprofits seeking to expand their audience and services. Writing a successful grant package requires numerous skills, including identifying and researching potential funders: following each grant makers' instructions; painting a persuasive picture in words and graphics; and integrating narrative and financial data into a dynamic proposal. In the hands of a qualified individual or team, grant writing is almost an art form. Creating a smooth process for grant writing, with a team of active and inspired people, is a necessity for today's future-focused nonprofits.

1. In this organization or elsewhere, tell about a time when you were successfully involved in requesting money or other resources. What made it successful? What did you know about the person or organization that helped you make a case for your request?

2. How has grant funding enhanced your organization's overall ability to function efficiently? If your organization is not currently funded by grants, how could grant funding enhance its overall ability to function efficiently?

3. If the future of your organization was dependent on securing grant funding and all hands were needed to prepare grant proposals, for what role would you volunteer? What knowledge, skills, personal experiences or passion would you bring to developing a proposal? What specific ideas would you want to see the proposal incorporate?

27.

A Party Where Everyone Is Clamoring to Donate

Hosting a benefit or fundraising event is one of the best ways to spread awareness about your organization while cultivating a source of unrestricted funding. Amazing fundraising events balance creativity, resources, careful planning and plenty of fun. At these events, donors feel committed to their involvement and acknowledged for their support. By celebrating a donor's dedication to your organization, its mission and vision, you nurture relationships and help secure future donations.

1. Tell me about the most effective fundraising event you witnessed, planned or read about. What made it great?

2. What do you value about the community of donors that supports your organization? What motivates them to donate? How could a fundraising event expand upon your organization's donor community?

3. Imagine your organization is hosting the largest, most successful, best-attended event it has ever given. What type of planning was involved? What role did you play? Who is in attendance? How are contributors recognized and acknowledged? What are donors saying about your organization and how they feel?

The Virtual World of Fundraising

We live in a wired and wireless world. Increasingly, nonprofits are leveraging the power of the internet and email for communicating and marketing their services and fundraising — with great success. An interesting website, showcasing services and accomplishments, is frequently an initial point of awareness for a potential donor or funder. The proliferation of email and the internet means that potential donors and funders may be reached instantaneously with timely and professional outreach efforts, thereby increasing opportunities to tap potential dollars.

1. Describe a marketing/fundraising campaign you were involved in — either inside or outside of work — where you donated money or other resources. What communications did you receive? How did the campaign excite you? What was the result for you?

2. What elements of the successful campaign were electronic? How could this campaign have taken even greater advantage of electronic messaging and requests? What elements would make it even more appealing to you?

3. Imagine a large-scale all-electronic fundraising outreach campaign for your organization. Be creative and imagine that the sky is the limit for executing electronic campaigns! What steps would your organization need to take to launch a successful electronic fundraising campaign? How do you keep electronic exchanges personal to retain a sense of face-to-face interaction with your pool of funders? What special points are you going to emphasize to make your organization stand out from the crowd?

29.

Telling the World Our Message

Organizations want their name mentioned when people are asked: "Who would you donate to if you had a million dollars?" In hopes of landing in such a position, nonprofits employ many methods of spreading the word about their services. A successful organization's marketing and public relations efforts capture the attention of donors by celebrating its community impact. By telling the world this organization is extraordinary, it makes the community proud to be part of its mission and inspires donors, volunteers and employees.

1. Tell me about an advertisement that got you excited about an organization and its product. What made it so inspiring or motivating? What feelings did it evoke? How did it contribute to you wanting to be a part of "the action"?

2. What do you see as key ideas that sell this organization, formally and informally?

3. What do you think you can contribute to the marketing campaign for this organization? What are the marketing and public relation elements — such as word of mouth, advertisements or email announcements — where you could make an impact?

4. Think of five phrases that describe this organization and give it meaning in the community. Imagine you are writing copy for a TV spot; each word costs money and must be potent.

5. Five years from now this organization has launched a successful marketing/public relations campaign about its tremendous work and impact on its targeted service recipients. The organization is getting recognized at an international conference acknowledging nonprofits. What is the name of the award? Why is this organization the award recipient? What steps led to this recognition?

30.

Our Name, Our Face, Our Place

To be successful, an organization carefully crafts the message that conveys the essence of what it is and what it does. An organization's identity is reflected in its logo, colors, language, mission statement and taglines, to name a few. The successful branding and marketing of its identity makes it a respected name, face and place — generating invaluable community support.

1. Tell me about an organization whose logo and mission immediately speaks to its purpose. What catches your eye or ear? What feelings does it generate?

2. Describe what you believe is the identity of your organization. How do its logo, tagline, mission and communication materials (print and web) reflect its work? What parts of your identity are most easily identified through its public messages?

3. You have been asked to join our organization's new community outreach campaign. The purpose is to leverage the organization's current logo, colors, message, mission statement and language. What recommendations would you make for this campaign's printed materials? Website and email marketing? What is the outcome of this well-executed outreach campaign?

31.

Marketing your Loyalty to Purpose

Outside support for an organization flows directly from its purpose. Organizations with successful marketing, public relations and outreach efforts utilize their purpose, accurately reflecting it in all their communications. In both words and actions, their messages are intentional; they target those most closely affected by their services. Communication becomes exponentially stronger when guided by the organization's purpose, mission, vision and values.

1. We have all encountered situations where we felt very strongly about being involved in a project that was clear about its purpose. Thinking about the myriad of organizations that ask for donations of time or money, describe one that was clear in its purpose and did a great job of defining it for others. What elements of those messages made you understand its purpose and what it was asking of you? How did the message make you feel?

2. What is your organization's purpose? What are some key words or phrases that tell the community what you are about and why? How is this reflected in your organization's marketing and PR campaigns or messages?

3. Imagine your organization is being honored in the community as a nonprofit that has modeled its purpose. List several key phrases that describe your purpose. Under each phrase describe actions that your organization took to meet each purpose. Describe strategies for creating and disseminating your messages to your constituencies.

32.

Principles of Partnership

Organizations that unite, strengthen and enhance services in the broader community. Seeing each other as valued partners allows for recognition of respective contributions. In successful collaborations, each partner has a voice and is thanked for the contributions it makes. Conversations are respectful and all of the voices are heard and understood. Compassion and a collaborative spirit — reflected in words and actions — inspire all to do more for the community they serve.

1. Reflecting on your experience, describe a time when you partnered with one or more people to complete a project – this could be from a locally-designed school bake sale to a city-wide effort to operate a recycling center. What are some principles or values that made the experience a positive and productive one? What contributions made you most proud of and satisfied with the partnership?

2. Describe a time when your organization partnered with another agency(ies) to enhance services for the community you serve.
    • What was the purpose of the project? Who were the other agencies involved? Who benefited from the partnership?
    • What made the partnership and the project successful?
    • What strategies did the partners use to create unity, shared understanding and a common purpose?

3. Dream into the future…Three years from now numerous organizations have successfully partnered to enhance their The

services. What are the issues that have improved as a result of the partnership? In a speech talking about this collaboration, identify three to five underlying principles that enabled each partner to feel it shared in a "win-win" partnership.

33.

Everyone Wins with Partnerships

Partners joined together in the spirit of cooperation and generosity create possibilities for a collective dream that inspires a new future, expanded resources and increased services. Shared perspective, creativity, wisdom and resources culminate in mutually beneficial outcomes. In contributing to the partnership and the collective dream, everyone wins.

1. Tell me a story about when you engaged in a partnership that generated extraordinary results — one where all partners benefited. This could be an inter-agency collaboration or a personal experience. What was the dream? Who were the partners? How did the process evolve? What were the outcomes?

2. Explain why the partnership produced greater results than a single source could provide.

3. Tell me about the most memorable experience in this endeavor. What did you value most about the opportunity to partner with others?

4. If, tomorrow, your organization begins forming a mutually beneficial partnership, what and who might be involved? What might the partnership provide? Who benefits? Describe how you see yourself contributing.

5. Imagine that your partnership group is selected to present at a national conference portraying your highly successful project. You are presenting before an audience that has not yet experienced the spirit of partnership. How would you convince them that partnering creates abundance? Share the top three benefits of partnering that will inspire them to co-create their own dream project.

34.

Building Community through Integrated Funding

In today's economy it's rare to have all of the money needed to run an organization, much less having it come from one source. Integrating funding to support mutually-aligned activities helps create adequate financial resources to carry out an organization's mission. Successful organizations weave, blend and braid funds with relative ease; they are champions of thinking outside the financial box so that everyone benefits.

1. Think about a time in your personal or work life where you were part of a shared-money partnership that contributed to a fulfilling and exciting end product. What made it so satisfactory? What did you understand about how your money was utilized? How did you benefit? How did a partner benefit?

2. What skills, talents and values can you bring to the concept of collaboration around funding? What excites you about being part of such an endeavor?

3. You are standing in line in a grocery store waiting to check out. A person you haven't seen in several years asks about how your organization is doing in these "tight financial times." What do you say about the benefits of partnering? What will you say to assist others to "catch the bug" of a true integrated-funding partnership

4. You are reading <u>The Grantsmanship Center Journal</u> five years from now and an article highlights your organization as a model for braided funding, partnering and collaboration. What does the article say about how the organization achieved this goal? How do all the participating agencies feel about this recognition?

35.

Maintaining Identities in Partnerships

Successful collaborations can occur between any two or more willing, dedicated and unique parties. Organizations driven towards creating more services, new ideas and a stronger understanding of similar agencies, build a network of allies. They successfully collaborate while each maintains its distinct character. Great things happen when partners share precious resources while honoring each partner's separate, viable and respected identity. The benefits to partnering in this way are twofold; sharing helps partners to work more efficiently and stretches meager assets.

1. What characteristics about yourself do you value? How do these play into your identity? How does it feel when others recognize and affirm you?

2. Think about a situation (personal or work related) when your "identity" was blended with another "identity." How did this happen? How did it feel? What were the benefits?

3. As we contemplate successful organizational collaboration that will expand services and resources, name one agency that might be a likely partner. What is important to that agency? How might you ensure this partner feels respected and can retain its identity? What can it do for you that will maintain your organization's identity?

4. Imagine it is five years later and you are part of a panel discussion talking about successful partnering. What are key

82

aspects of your agency that are still intact and functioning well? What about the partner agency? How has each organization's identity been retained? Enhanced? How are services better?

36.

Researching Donors

Cultivating donors begins with identifying a connection between the donor and the organization seeking support. Donations are derived from relationships, either personal or business. Research provides vital information for targeting potential donors — be they foundations, businesses or individuals. This research forms the basis for fruitful relationships with contributors where both the donor and the recipient organization benefit. Foundations usually have targeted areas they support. Businesses may glean a reciprocal benefit from affiliation with you. Individual donors often have a history with your organization or support a specific need.

1. Tell me about why you donate time, money, or energy to a specific organization or cause. Describe how it meets your personal needs and values. How does it make you feel?

2. Describe your experiences in working with donors or seeking donations in any setting. If they were successful, what happened and why? What special research did you do? If in hindsight, you could have done something differently, what might it have been?

3. How are donations sought in your current organization? If it tries to target specific donors by developing relationships, how is that done?

4. Imagine your organization has a phenomenal record for securing lasting donations, either endowments or yearly contributions you can count on. Describe the activities your organization undertook to make this possible. What key elements contributed to your success?

37.

Reaching Donors

For a donor, gift giving provides a deep sense of satisfaction, fulfillment and shared values. Generally, people "give back" to communities and/or organizations that meet their interests or needs. They often feel a connection to the work of the organization and the community it serves. Showing that you understand donors, acknowledging their relationship to your purpose and recognizing their generosity inspires donors to continue a long-term relationship with your organization — one that may secure your future for years to come.

1. Think of the first time you gave a gift to an organization. What energized you? What did the organization do that encouraged your gift? How did you feel before, during and after your donation?

2. What are an organization's essential aspects that must be in place prior to your choice to give a gift? What keeps you energized to continue giving to an organization? How do you feel after making your contribution?

3. Thinking about your organization, describe its contributions to the community. What groups of people would likely donate to the organization and consequently build long-term giving relationships? How can we most effectively tap their resources?

4. Dream into the future...your organization has had long standing success with securing donors' monetary and emotional support. You have asked one of your donors to address your annual meeting and to talk about his/her

experience in giving to the organization. What does that donor say about your organization? About his/her commitment to your work?

38.

Donors' Commitment to Community

One of the most compelling reasons why donors make gifts is to thank and "give back" to a community that has been good to them and/or their families. Once the gift is made, a donor not only feels a sense of personal fulfillment but also that he or she is providing for future generations. A commitment to his/her community ensures a sense of personal satisfaction for the donor while providing vital funding to an organization.

1. Think about the first time you, or someone you know, made a major gift to an organization. Tell me about the experiences you had with this organization prior to the giving. Why did you choose that particular organization? What made this gift-giving special for you?

2. Now focus on the current organization(s) to which you give a financial gift. What are the connections that helped you to select this organization? How do you like to be approached when an organization is requesting a major contribution? What are the elements that encourage you to give to an organization? What would you like in return for your contribution?

3. Imagine it is five years from now and you have received the Community Support Award for community giving. What did you do to receive this award? How did you decide where to give your donations? How has your gift improved your community? How can you use this award to encourage others to get involved through giving or volunteering for the community?

39.

Donor Connections Count

Fortunately, donors donate! Without the charitable donations of individuals and businesses many nonprofit organizations would cease to exist. Donors are crucial for organizations, but nonprofit organizations serve a function for donors as well. Donors probably have a past, present or future relationship with the organization that is important to them. Often, a donation is a way of honoring the donor's connection to the organization. Identifying that connection and the reasons for donating are important first steps in understanding why donors donate and in cultivating a lasting relationship.

1. Think about the donations you routinely make in your personal life. What are your reasons for donating to various organizations or causes?

2. Think about the donors to your current nonprofit organization. Why do you think they donate? How would you describe the different reasons for foundation, business and personal donations?

3. How does your organization cultivate donors? What are the connections? How does it identify potential new donors?

4. Imagine you are in charge of fundraising and donations for your organization. You are being publicly recognized for your exemplary work. During your acceptance speech, what will you say about the importance of donations to your organization? What will you say about your donors?

40.

Honoring Dedicated Donors

Recognition is one of the most important factors in keeping an organization's donors vested in building long-term relationships. Donors sustain their commitment when they feel "valued" by the organization. Long-time, repeat donors are the most important building block for a charitable organization's long-term success. Consequently, a strong donor appreciation and recognition program is an important, albeit often overlooked, factor in a charitable organization's success. The savvy organization has crafted donor recognition plans tailored to the donor's needs.

1. Think of the first time you were part of an organization that recognized a person or group. What contacts were made prior, during and after the recognition? What did the recognition look like? Did your organization recognize this person, or group, a second time? If so, how did the second time differ from the first?

2. Describe how your donor recognition program functions today. How do you customize your recognition to the donor's needs?

3. Five years from today you pick up your daily newspaper and see that your organization received national recognition for its donor appreciation program. Describe your donor recognition program. What happened in five years to help your organization win this award? What do donors say about your recognition program?

41.

Tapping the Passionate Volunteers

Volunteers are vital assets to organizations. They are special people with a special calling who bring their passions to the organizations they serve. Dedicated volunteers are challenged and have opportunities to experience growth. They bring passion to their tasks and deserve to feel good about their donation of time and energy.

Volunteer recruitment plans are as creative and dynamic as the people an organization wants to attract. They shout, "Passionate volunteers wanted!! We embrace our volunteers and their passions, support success and reward their time, talents and energies."

1. Describe a personally satisfying volunteer experience. What motivated you to do this volunteer work? How were you treated and what kept you engaged?

2. Looking at your organization, what strategies has it used to recruit volunteers successfully? What would volunteers say enticed them to your organization?

3. What has your role been in working with successful volunteers? How do you make volunteering for your organization appealing? How do your volunteers know they are appreciated for their talents, time and energy?

4. We want potential volunteers to know that "at this organization your passions will be tapped and appreciated." What future

actions can your organization do to convey this important message? What will volunteers see, hear, feel and experience when they are working with you?

42.

The Spice of Volunteer Life

Great volunteers are a key ingredient in many nonprofits' success. Organizations reap benefits for years to come by spending time and energy on sustaining committed, energetic volunteers. Long-term volunteers often cite feeling valued and knowing their work is meaningful as reasons for continued dedication. Creating an organizational structure that attracts and supports its volunteers ensures a dedicated non-paid workforce.

1. Describe a volunteer experience you've had and tell me about what personal needs were met. What training did you receive? How did you benefit?

2. Reflect on how volunteers "fit" with the efforts of accomplishing your organization's mission. What makes them important to your work?

3. Think about the most motivated volunteers with whom you have worked. What fueled their passion? How were personal needs of the volunteers met?

4. Imagine you are contributing in a volunteer capacity at a nonprofit agency. Describe its impressive volunteer support and recognition system. What is done on a daily, weekly and periodic basis to keep volunteers energized? What types of support are in place?

43.

Joy In Volunteer Work

Volunteer work often differs from paid positions in that motivation stems from a desire to contribute, to feel good about giving, to enhance a personal experience and/or to belong to a fun group of new friends. These "extras" serve as non-monetary compensation for contributions of time and energy. Creating volunteer environments peppered with fun often provides an especially appealing non-monetary benefit. Engaged and joyful volunteers exude a sense of happiness and delight. Motivated, they work hard while having fun.

1. Tell me a story about the most fun you ever had while working. What were the activities and who were the people involved? What made it fun?

2. What do you value about your organization's ability to have fun? What emotional and social benefits come from your work? Talk about how volunteers are, or could be, involved in the fun.

3. A year from now your organization has made it a priority to maintain a fun working environment for all volunteers. What fun things has your organization implemented that specifically include your hard-working volunteers? How do you know the volunteers are more motivated and getting more work done?

44.

Synergy Among Staff and Volunteers

When an office has synergy among employees and volunteers, everyone feels it! The organization is pulsing and the mix of staff and volunteers keeps the organization strong. Nurturing that positive energy is work worth doing. Valuing the contributions and creating opportunities for staff and volunteer collaborations keeps project ideas fresh and innovative and volunteers engaged and energized.

1. Tell me about a successful project you worked on with both employees and volunteers. How did staff and volunteers coordinate efforts? What made it a success? What were the benefits to all involved?

2. What do you value most about working with volunteers on projects? What might they add that wouldn't otherwise be included?

3. Assume you are the lead on a major project involving an equal mix of staff and volunteers. How will you coordinate the two to ensure success? How will you make certain that the contribution of each group is recognized?

4. Three years from now your organization has developed a program to ensure that volunteers and staff are working together in a cooperative and productive manner. What steps has the agency taken to help with this process? How is it different than what was happening at the beginning of the program? What strategies promote communication and productivity? How do employees and volunteers feel?

The Care and Development of Volunteers

Excellent organizations give as much thought to the preparation, training and development of volunteers as they do for their paid staff. Thoughtfulness ensures volunteers feel their time and energy is well-used and meaningful. Organizations that keep the care and development of volunteers high on the priority list manifest an active and dedicated volunteer crew.

1. Think about an excellent work orientation experience you have had. Describe this experience. What made it memorable? How did you feel about the work you did?

2. Thinking about your organization's current volunteer orientation, describe the process. What happens when they arrive? What training is provided prior to, or during, their volunteer time? What supports are available to them when they have questions or seek direction?

3. Dream into the future…your sole responsibility is to design and implement a volunteer program for your agency. Resources are not an issue. How do you welcome volunteers to your organization? What orientation and ongoing training opportunities do you provide? What kinds of work do they do? How are they supervised and supported?

4. What aspects of this dream can you implement immediately? What next steps will you take to make the experience valuable for volunteers and the organization?

46.

Rewarding Valued Volunteers

Volunteers are dedicated individuals who give up precious time to benefit an organization. An unknown author has said, "People will forget what you said, people will forget what you did, but they will never forget how you made them feel." Letting volunteers know their time, energy and talents are appreciated ensures their continued commitment. Rewards come in all shapes and sizes: for example, a thank you, gift certificates, volunteer parties, recognition certificates or
mention in the next newsletter. A corps of talented volunteers is inspiring; a talented–and appreciated–corps of volunteers is priceless.

1. What is the value that volunteers bring to this organization?

2. Tell me about a time when volunteers influenced the outcome of a project/effort at this organization. What did they do? How were they recognized or rewarded for that effort?

3. Imagine it is two years from now and you have worked with a team to develop a volunteer rewards and recognition program. What is the title of this program? What are the key elements? How are volunteers evaluated, recognized and/or rewarded? What feedback have you received from volunteers about the program?

47.

Who Do We Serve?

Nonprofits are in business to serve a particular population and purpose, as defined in their bylaws. Recipients or members are the particular group benefiting from its services. Whether in the context of community nonprofits or professional associations, defining a nonprofit's particular constituency helps target services and allocate resources.

1. Tell me a story about a specific client or customer who benefited from your services. How did that client fit into the organization's service structure? How did you know this? Would the person also have been able to benefit from another organization? If so, how did the client or member decide on your organization to meet his/her needs?

2. Think about your current nonprofit organization. Describe the client base. Who do you serve and why? If a person has several options to choose from, what is unique about your organization? What specific needs do you meet?

3. You are preparing a one paragraph description of this organization's service recipients or its membership. What are five positive phrases that illustrate who you are serving and five that communicate the services offered?

4. An organization should periodically review who it serves. How would you do this?

48.

Hearing Their Call

Relevant nonprofit organizations meet the needs of the population they serve, but the needs of recipients or members may be different today than several years ago. Successful nonprofits *intentionally and regularly* reconsider their clientele's needs. "Hearing the call" and "responding" to it are keys to aligning the organization's work with the stated needs of its recipients/members.

1. Tell me a story about a time when you successfully requested help from another person or organization that met a significant need. This might be something at work or in your personal life, such as customer service or a personal crisis. What did it feel like to ask for help? How did you make it known? What were encouraging responses from the person or organization that helped you?

2. What are the needs you hear about from the recipients of your current nonprofit organization? How do you get that information — formally and informally? How is the information accumulated, shared and used to improve services?

3. Think of a need a service recipient or member might express. Describe the "perfect" response your organization could make. Money, time and resources being of no consequence, what would be the ultimate success?

4. You are writing a plan for getting accurate and up-to-date

information from the people you serve. What strategies would you include, using both formal and informal activities? What barriers may get in the way and how can you address them to make the effort successful?

49.

Community Feedback Feeds Growth

Organizations see themselves as experts about the community they serve. What they might not know, however, is how they are viewed by the community. Devising methods for evaluating the community's perception of an organization guides the direction of its future work. It also provides a forum for open-ended dialogue among all community organizations, stimulating fresh approaches for continued growth and needed change.

1. Think about another organization with which your agency or association has or should have a working relationship. If you were asked to give feedback on its services to the population you work with, what would you say?
   - What are its strengths?
   - What suggestions would you make to better its services?
   - How would you feel about being asked?
   - After you have given this information, what feedback would you like from them?

2. Which organizations and individuals within your "community" would be important to contact and ask for feedback? Why did you pick them? What might you expect to hear as strengths? As areas for improvement?

3. Consider you are part of a team creating a comprehensive plan for soliciting feedback on your services from other community organizations that work with similar constituent groups. What methods would you suggest? What recommendations do you

have about necessary questions? Create a sample introduction for this effort.

4. How do you imagine this feedback will impact your organization and the community you serve?

50.

Winning Teamwork Around our Mission

Successful nonprofit organizations have a variety of strategies to encourage teamwork and a sense of community. Work settings that welcome and spark creativity keep teams fresh and lively as they go about sustaining an organization's mission. Quality comes when people at all levels of an organization pool ideas, talents and skills toward improving results aligned with their stated mission.

1. Think about a job or situation where everyone worked toward a common purpose. Tell me about the people involved. How did the mission or purpose of the group encourage everyone to work successfully together? What was your role in supporting this flourishing working relationship?

2. What personal values do you carry into your teamwork? How do you benefit? What characteristics, talents and skills do you contribute?

3. In your current work setting, how is creativity inspired by the mission and purpose of the organization? What are the elements that utilize everyone's creativity and talents? How do teams effectively work together?

4. Think ahead five years. Within this nonprofit, all of the individuals are creatively inspired by the organization's mission and engaged in mutually satisfying teamwork. What motivated everyone to rally around the mission? What was your role? How has teamwork benefited your organization and your clients?

51.

Reflecting our Diverse World

Like a quilt, organizations and groups are woven with a variety of fabrics. The more varied the fabrics are in size, color, texture, length and age, the more interesting and complete a quilt appears. Yet, no matter how many different combinations, a common thread stitches the quilt together to create one strong, lasting piece.

Our world has never been so small! A great and growing quilt, the United States gains strength form its diversity, from its people of various races, genders, religions, ability, sexual orientation, age, income levels and/or cultures. Leaders and staff within nonprofit organizations are most effective when they reflect those varied groups. Through diversity we discover and embrace our commonalities, threading together a strong, resilient and comfortable structure: a magnificent quilt that reflects community life.

1. Reflect on a time you were a minority in a group. Describe the experience and the accompanying feelings. Did you feel the "leadership" in the situation was speaking for you and/or reflecting your views? How did this make you feel?

2. Think about your current nonprofit organization. Describe the diversity of the recipients of your services? Describe the diversity of your staff and leadership (Board, CEO, managers). What strengths can a more diverse staff and leadership bring to your organization?

3. How can you personally promote diversity within your organization's staff and leadership? How can commonalities among diverse peoples be highlighted and celebrated?

4. Imagine a future where you work in an organization that reflects the diversity of people the organization serves. What do you see on the walls, in the structure of the office and in the publications of that organization? How do people relate to one another in the office and outside the workplace? What do your service recipients say about the organization?

Three Cheers for Staff

Nonprofits are fortunate in that they generally attract staff who have a passion for the organization's cause(s) and who believe in the work they do. Acknowledging these dedicated employees stimulates staff retention and morale. Developing a recognition process that demonstrates sincere appreciation is key to letting staff know they matter. Employee recognition can be spontaneous and informal, or intentional and formal; what matters is that staff receive "hoorahs" for their dedication and contributions.

1. Tell me about the best award, reward or recognition you received in any situation? What did you do to earn that award? What made it special for you? What was said to you? How did it make you feel?

2. What positive staff recognitions occur at your current job? What are the elements of a recognition that are most important?

3. Imagine it's a year from today. You have been instrumental in developing a new program that brought enhanced services to the community your organization serves. Your work is being honored at an important event. Tell me what you see happening at that event. What happens prior to the event? Who is invited to the ceremony and why are they included? What happens after the event? How do you feel?

4. What ideas would you contribute to a committee formed to implement a thoughtful and intentional staff recognition program for your organization? What are the positive effects you envision this committee having?

53.

Bountiful Benefits

Wages and salary do not tell the whole story! Both profit and nonprofit entities boost the employee base pay through benefit packages. Nonprofits have discretion as to the benefits they provide, particularly those that do not have significant monetary impact or are regulated by the IRS. For many employees, non-monetary benefits include flex-time, gym discounts, on-site child care and "cafeteria" plans. These tremendously enhance an employee's quality of life. Organizations that seek input from staff and provide flexibility and choices certainly provide bountiful benefits.

1. Describe a work environment you, a family member, or friend experienced that had bountiful benefits? What were those benefits? Why did you consider them so great? What did the benefits reflect about the organization and its values?

2. What is the best part of your current benefits? If you could add something to your current benefit package, what would that be? How would it help you?

3. What is the best bountiful benefit package, both monetary and non-monetary you can imagine? How would these benefits affect your professional and personal outlook? What impact would your new outlook have on your organization?

54.

To Stay or Go?

Cultivating a positive work environment, rich with meaning and full of challenges, encourages staff retention and makes an organization the "right place to be for me." Most employees prefer to stay with a job for as long as possible. Still, many factors influence their decision to "stay or go." Successful organizations recognize these factors and strive to keep employees engaged in — and rewarded for — their work.

1. Tell me about your most rewarding and engaging job/project, either work-related or personal. What were you doing? Who were you working with? Why did it feel so good?

2. Tell me about your current position. How long have you been working here? What kinds of things do you do? What ingredients of this job motivate you to stay? What more could your organization do to keep you happy?

3. Describe an experience where you felt your personal values were reflected in your work.

4. Three years from now you are a supervisor of 12 people. You have a staff person who has been offered a position with another organization for slightly more money, but basically doing the same kind of work. You have asked that person into your office to discuss the decision. The person tells you that he/she has decided to stay, largely because of you. What does this person say about how you contributed to his/her retention? What do you learn from this conversation about what motivates and retains employees?

55.

Culturally Competent Workplaces Create Success

Organizations that effectively communicate with their diverse customers, employees, partners and communities are models of cultural competence and true success. Cultural competence focuses on *"inclusivity"* that recognizes and values the diverse backgrounds, experiences and assets of all people. As our population becomes more ethnically, culturally and racially diverse, so does the workforce. Fostering work environments rich with cross-cultural teams adds luster to all you do. Modeling cultural competence within and outside of an organization exemplifies the future where diversity is the welcomed norm.

1. Talk about a time you experienced a culturally competent organization. How did the staff and people work together? Think broadly in terms of culture: Who was represented? What elements encouraged them to work together? What was your role in supporting this successful working relationship?

2. Now, look at your organization and tell me how your organization is culturally competent. How do people support each other in cultural competence? What systems encourage cultural understanding and learning? What elements encourage everyone to work effectively together?

3. Five years from now, your organization has been named one of the top ten most diverse and best places to work. Visualize all your co-workers successfully working together. What policies

and expectations achieved this recognition? What did every one within your organization do to reach this point? What was your role? Give me two examples of how employees from diverse backgrounds work together and have learned from one another.

56.

Leaders Inspiring High Performers

In the last 30 years management theory shifted from an outdated command and control paradigm to one of trust and freedom. Today's supervisors and managers utilize a variety of methods for encouraging staff development, including clarity of expectations, feedback, acknowledgements, training, designing work around whole tasks and coaching and mentoring. Stellar organizations (profit, nonprofit, or governmental agencies) foster employee competence, confidence, creativity and accountability aligned with the organization's vision and goals. Competent, confident staff allow leaders to focus on guiding their organizations to the next level and beyond.

1. Tell me about a time when a leader's efforts fostered commitment and high performance in an organization. What happened? How did leaders bring out the best in people? Personally, what did you experience in this situation? How did you feel?

2. Describe a situation when performance and commitment were at their peak in your organization. What were the circumstances? What was leadership's role? What, specifically, did leadership do to inspire the commitment? What part did you play?

3. Your organization makes a three-year plan for inspiring high performance from all its members.
   - What will the leadership's role be in achieving this goal?
   - How will leaders and employees interact to ensure forward progression?
   - How will this workplace feel in three years?

110

57.

Kindling Motivation

The hum of workers busily involved and happily engaged in their work is music to a manager's ears. When employees have high motivation they are self-starters and good problem solvers. When their energy is highly charged, innovative ideas sizzle. When the fires of motivation are kindled, the glow from employee dedication and commitment radiates throughout the organization. Motivated staff approach work with a lively passion and see themselves as a vital part of the organization's purpose. Their work– and that of the organization–holds greater meaning and value.

1. Tell me a story about a project where you were totally motivated and inspired. How did it feel? What contributed to the motivation? What were the rewards of the effort?

2. Describe a time when many employees were highly motivated on a project. What was happening? How did it feel to be part of the project? What sparks created this environment? What was your role? How were others responding? What did the organization gain?

3. Tell me what motivates you. What gets your energy ignited?

4. What do you value about yourself as a motivator?

5. Your organization's leadership asked you to help formulate a plan for enhancing staff motivation. How do you define motivation? What three actions do you suggest? What needs to happen to make implementation effective?

58.

Defining Talent Needs

Identifying and nurturing individual talents has the potential to benefit an organization by garnering happy and productive staff. Talent encompasses a consistent pattern of behavior that defines a person and illuminates his/her best. Recognizing the natural talents people bring to their work breeds success for the employee and the organization. When work accurately matches a person's talents, the product becomes exponentially stronger. Build a team focused on tasks, aligned with their natural gifts and watch for amazing outcomes!

1. Tell me a story about a situation where you felt fulfilled and productive, where coming to work or engaging in an outside activity was a joy. What were the requirements of the job or activity? What talents did you bring? How were your talents used?

2. We all have talents to contribute. How do your talents differ from those of your colleagues? How do your talents complement your colleagues? How could your special talents be used more effectively?

3. Develop two to three interview questions that would help potential employers identify the talents that prospective employees bring.

59.

Feedback Encouraging Superior Performance

People generally arrive at work intending to be high performers, whether working for pay or as a volunteer. Superior performance is promoted when expectations are clear and training and resources support their work. Once these are in place, ongoing feedback is the mechanism that sustains continued growth, goal-setting and accountability. To be effective, feedback must be clear, sufficient and appropriate to the task. Effective feedback challenges people to grow in their jobs and contribute to the overall achievement of the organization's goals.

1. Tell a story of a time when you knew you were doing good work in line with the organization's goals. What was your role? What feedback did you receive? How did it feel? How could feedback have been even better to make more of an impact?

2. Describe your job and what milestones or targets let you know you are doing your work on time and well. What training and resources have been most helpful to you? What feedback do you receive? What additional information would be beneficial to help you produce your best work?

3. Imagine a future when your organization is breaking all records for accomplishing its intended goals. What ongoing feedback did each person receive? Describe the manner in which it was given — its frequency and tone and the methods used. What feedback strategies do you feel are most effective and why?

113

60.

Reflective Supervision

Reflective supervision is a relationship for learning. Using reflective conversations, a supervisor assists employees in thinking about his/her attitudes and behaviors and applying insight and knowledge to enhance professional competence. It is a strengths-based, mutually respectful and collaborative approach to supervision. It presents an environment of intellectual inquiry, open communications, emotional safety and empathy with staff concerns. In addition to being reflective, this method of supervision is collaborative and conducted regularly.

Reflective supervision models support and respect for a supervisee's decision-making. This model is especially potent in agencies dealing directly with clients. Bringing one's own work situation to a supervisor, the supervisor listens to the supervisee, assisting the person to share and use self-reflection to problem-solve. The anticipated result — an employee who uses, with clients, the same reflective model as the supervisor has modeled.

1. Recall a time in a working situation when you felt heard and respected and engaged in your own problem-solving. Describe the helpful interactions. How did you grow and develop from that situation? How has it affected the way you do your job now?

2. Your organization is being recognized as one of your city's ten best places to work — the category is "employee growth and learning." You are asked to speak at a luncheon about the

reflective practices that bolstered your professional development. Describe five things about your relationship with your supervisor that inspired your continued development.

3. Your organization is considering utilizing "reflective supervision" with direct service staff — those who interact with clients regularly. As a manager or supervisor what help would you need to use this approach?

61.

Valuing Peace in Our Workplaces

Our world would be harmonious if we spent more time focusing on "peace" rather than "conflict." Whether in international relations, schools, homes, businesses or our nonprofit organizations, we all have the opportunity to focus our efforts on promoting peace and harmony rather than war and disagreement. Organizations benefit from talking about how to promote peace, peaceful solutions and a peaceful atmosphere. Modern organizations have the unique opportunity to define and model peaceful approaches in their daily and long-term goals.

1. What comes to mind when you hear the word "peace?" What feelings are evoked? What are the mental images you have? Share some examples of where you currently promote peace in your life situations.

2. How do you see yourself bringing peaceful traits to the workplace? Talk about a potential conflict situation and how you might reframe it by adopting peaceful solutions.

3. Describe how your commitment to peace would be applied to a situation where you have to discipline a staff person for poor performance, or something more severe such as sexual harassment?

4. Imagine you are leading your organization to be an exemplary model of valuing peace. What would be your slogan or motto? Why this particular motto or slogan?

62.

Delegating the Right Jobs to the Right People

Although delegating is a powerful tool for a leader to use, it can also be a difficult skill to master. Many successful projects are the result of a team whose leader determined the strengths of each member and assigned tasks accordingly. Effective delegation of tasks means the right job has been placed into the hands of the right person. The result: everyone feels they've contributed to the organization's success, no matter how large or small their task!

1. Tell me about a time you successfully led a team through a daunting task by delegating to your team members. What did you need to know about people to make good delegating decisions? How did you make decisions about work assignments? How did you convey this message to the various workers?

2. Tell me about a past situation where you *now see* you could have had better results by delegating tasks differently. What would be different about the situation today and/or your role?

3. Imagine a future where the world is filled with skilled employees and delegating managers. You are observing this scenario as an outsider. What does this look like? How are workers interacting? How is accountability assured? What is the result?

63.

Creating the "Ideal" Employee

The dream of every supervisor is to have a staff of "ideal" employees. However, all supervisors and colleagues have different criteria in mind when using the phrase "model" employee." Very often job descriptions and performance appraisals list tasks without addressing less tangible values and behaviors that contribute to great employees. Excellent supervisors articulate the characteristics that are important, meld them into the tasks expected, model these important traits, create a work environment that promotes "model" employee behavior and utilize a recognition or reward system that sustains the efforts.

1. Tell me about a time you saw yourself as a model employee. What did you do that made you so valuable? How did you know you were performing well? How were you recognized or rewarded?

2. If you have supervised staff, describe an "ideal" employee. What values, characteristics and behaviors do you expect from such an individual?

3. As you think about those values, characteristics and behaviors, project into the future and describe how you can create an environment that supports your "ideal" employee. What would the workplace look like? What can you say and do? How can your feedback and coaching promote these concepts?

4. What are some initial actions that you could take immediately to develop "ideal" employees in this organization? What steps does the organization have to take to support this effort?

Work Environments that Work

Organizations are like newlyweds on a budget: constantly challenged to do more with fewer resources. Successful managers create work environments where staff members feel good about themselves — and their surroundings — and thus motivate staff to produce positive results. Building work environments that satisfy individual needs, both physically and emotionally, nurtures a positive work culture for everyone and produces extraordinary results.

1. Describe a time when you worked in a positive environment. Who was involved? What was your role? What made the environment positive?

2. What do you value most about the culture and climate of your current work? How does this work environment make you feel alive, effective in your work and proud of your involvement?

3. Imagine opening the newspaper five years from now and seeing your organization on the front page for having the best work environment in the United States. What does the work environment look like? What do your co-workers say about the environment? What supports the positive atmosphere? What is your role in making this a positive work place?

65.

In the Communication Loop

Organizations function dynamically when everyone feels they are an equal link in the communication chain. Having information and "being in the loop" are important components for employee satisfaction. When "go-to" people are clearly identified and all employees know where to direct questions and/or feedback, the entire organization benefits. In a harmonious work zone, all employees feel valued and part of the communication loop because the "how's" and "what's" of information sharing are clearly defined.

1. Tell me about a time you experienced communication that was clear and exchanged in ways that felt meaningful. How were people sharing information among themselves, across teams and organization-wide? What structures/systems were in place to foster information sharing?

2. Describe how it felt to be a member of an organization where communication occurred at all levels. What was the impact on your work and that of others?

3. Imagine a future where communication is a cornerstone of your organization. What does this look like? Who are the key players? What is shared? What methods are used?
   What creates regularity and continuity of information sharing? How does this positively affect the culture of the organization?

66.

Clear, Sincere and Respectful Communication

Healthy and open communication is a necessary component of successful working relationships. Clear and respectful interactions foster a rich environment where people feel comfortable and free to communicate about everything — from difficult issues to small, everyday job annoyances. Employees feel a sense of personal and professional empowerment by being trusted to communicate on all issues and having their views treated with respect.

1. Describe a situation where a team you belonged to modeled healthy, open communication. How was it healthy? What was open? How did this impact the outcomes of your work?

2. Describe a situation in your current organization where open dialogue benefited you and the organization. How did that feel?

3. Imagine a year from now that a local television channel features your organization as a model for assuring that communications are clear, sincere and respectful at all levels. Share some "talking points" you have developed on these questions.
   - What is different now from this time last year?
   - What steps did your organization take to reach this goal?
   - How have you responded to the changes? How have those around you responded?

67.

A Learning Organization Just Keeps Rolling Along

Like an ocean, nonprofit organizations ebb and flow with the movements of society. In healthy, vibrant organizations, each member is continually expanding his/her knowledge and skills to usher in the continuous transformations dictated by changing funding, community interests and priorities. Continuous learning initiatives enhance collective capabilities and promote a productive, fresh and enthusiastic organization.

1. An organization supporting continuous learning creates an atmosphere where people feel they are stretching and growing while enhancing their ability to perform. Tell me a story about a time when you had to "stretch and grow" to accomplish your job? How did you do this? Who supported you and how? How did you feel upon learning new skills or knowledge?

2. Explain how "stretching and growing" affected others around you. What was said or done to indicate your learning had an impact on others? How did their comments or actions make you feel?

3. In what areas, topics or skills would you most like to expand your learning and why?

4. Describe what an organization that supports continuous learning looks like. What policies are in place? What organizational structure lends support to this effort? What are the benefits to the employees and to the organization?

122

68.

Lively Environments

When an organization has cultivated a lively environment it shows. Humor is a welcome office fixture. Laughter spills into the halls. People take an interest in one another that goes beyond an ordinary work interaction. The office is buzzing with energy because everyone has fun interacting with colleagues. This energy creates a juicy environment ripe for productivity and lasting results.

1. When have you been a part of a "juicy" team or office? Why was your work so much fun? What did the workplace look and feel like? How did the positive and enjoyable work relations impact your productivity and your motivation?

2. What personal values does a lively and energizing work environment meet for you? What can you contribute to creating that environment?

3. Imagine two years from now your organization is recognized as the year's liveliest work environment. What makes it so "lively" and productive? What does it look like? What does it feel like to be a part of this office? What did the organization do to help make it happen? How did you contribute?

69.

Cultivating Mutual Support Networks

Support networks are a critical component to everyday lives — most of us need them and are lucky when they're present in the workplace. Today's successful organizations build the concept of mutual support into their work culture. Knowing that co-workers are there to lend a hand, an ear, or a pat on the back makes a world of difference, fostering a work culture of generosity and compassion that leads to success.

1. Tell me a story of when you successfully engaged in a task with others where you helped each other and all benefited from the experience. How were others involved? What did they contribute? How did it feel to have support? How did the outcome of the task benefit from the support?

2. When you think about a mutually supportive work environment, what personal values do you have that would contribute to its success?

3. Think of a time when you knew you were experiencing and giving support on a major work project. Describe the experience, including the tasks, your feelings and the outcomes.

4. Assume you are part of a team chosen to create a model "supportive work environment." Describe the final model? What would you contribute to this model? What part does the organizational hierarchy play?

Living and Working our Values

Values are the deeply held beliefs that give meaning to our existence; that which we find worthwhile. They come from the heart, shape our behavior and give us direction. To meld our personal values into our daily work allows the organization to not only grow, but to blossom. When we truly believe in the work we do, we do it better — with extraordinary energy and results.

1. Talk about five values that are important to you. Why are they so important?

2. Tell me a story about an activity where you believed your work served an important purpose. Describe the setting and the energy level it produced. How did the activity reflect your values? How did you feel when engaged in the activity?

3. How does the organization help harness your values to your work?

4. Describe an ideal organization where values are integrated into the everyday work environment, promoting great energy and passion and thereby producing extraordinary results.

71.

Sharing the Credit

When everyone shares the credit for success, loyalty and satisfaction are nurtured and encouraged. The strength of an organization is derived from positive, happy and appreciated employees, board members, donors, community allies and volunteers. The entire organization benefits from creating a culture of acknowledgement — where everyone's contributions are appreciated.

1. Describe to me the various ways that success can be shared and acknowledged within an organization. What are the benefits to individuals and the organization?

2. Tell me about a time when you shared the credit for an accomplishment with a co-worker? How did this make you feel? How did sharing credit help or hurt your career, the organization or the perception of your colleagues?

3. Imagine you worked closely with a co-worker on a project. The co-worker was responsible for the project and gave a presentation to the president of your company. At the end of the presentation, your co-worker singled you out and highlighted your contributions. Following the presentation, the president personally thanked you. Describe what it felt like to receive this recognition from your co-worker and the president.

4. What are some ideas or suggestions you have to encourage your organization in "sharing the credit" — to make it a corporate expectation?

72.

Living a Balanced Life

Some people believe that true bliss is experienced through attaining and maintaining a life balance. Many of today's successful organizations recognize the need for a work/home balance and build it into their culture. Some have created alternative health options while others offer flexible work options to ease travel time and traffic headaches and many now provide employee gyms and child care. Finding the balance between work and the individual is a contemporary theme; striking that balance is likely the dream of many of today's busy people!

1. Tell me about the elements of your life that need to be kept in balance? Describe how you attempt to strike a balance. What works best? What is least successful? What strategies do you use to re-gain balance when it disappears from your life?

2. How could your organization help create more balance in your life? What would help? How could it be accomplished and be fair to all? What are you willing to do to support these ideas?

3. Assume that you are charged with developing a statement about creating a work/life balance. What would you say? What pictures or symbols might you use? What action steps could your organization's leadership take? How might encouraging balance improve the work climate?

73.

The Check *IS* in the Mail

One could say that financial resources do for businesses what gasoline does for automobiles — allows them to purr along. Just as automobiles rely on vendors to provide their fuel, businesses rely on vendors as partners to reach their goals. Private and public business owners, individuals, corporations and other providers of products and services are essential associates critical to an organization's success. To honor these obligations, responsive organizations create and implement efficient financial systems that assure: "The check IS in the mail" — by the promised date.

1. Tell me about a time you experienced a great sense of satisfaction working with an organization when you were expecting financial reimbursement or payment. What contributed to your satisfaction? How did the experience motivate you to work more closely with that organization?

2. As you think about your organization and its payment responsiveness and fiscal integrity, describe what you contribute to the organization's financial responsiveness. What would you like others to do? What will keep you inspired and active?

3. Two years have passed. Your organization has consistently been praised for its financial responsiveness and integrity by vendors. You are preparing an award for your fiscal department. What will you say about the staff and the systems in place? How have their efforts in being responsive benefited the entire organization? What aspects of your organizational culture nourished the staff's fiscal responsiveness and integrity?

The Checks and Balances of Fiscal Roles and Responsibilities

Implementing a system of checks and balances to maintain financial integrity is essential for organizations. Responsibility for financial accountability is crucial, especially since nonprofit financial resources normally require accountability to several funders. Effective finance departments ensure that every aspect of the organization's finances has a system of checks and balances. Formal approval processes that go through several levels of responsibility are essential in accounts payable and payroll functions, grant maintenance and reporting, cash receipts and bank reconciliations.

1. Consider the roles and responsibilities of everyone involved with financial management in your organization. How are tasks connected? Where does a separation of duties occur? What types of approval processes are in place to ensure more than one person looks at the department's various functions?

2. How could your organization improve upon its current system of checks and balances? What could non-financial people contribute? How might duties shift within the department assuring that no one person completely controls an entire function? How could the board of directors become more involved?

3. Think of what it would feel like to be certain that all financial functions contain sufficient checks and balances. How does this relate to the financial statements you produce, the audit reports you receive and the assurance of board members?

4. How could strict financial accountability make your organization more attractive to potential donors, volunteers or funding sources?

75.

Awesome Audit Reports

Financial audits are a company's "report card" presenting a window to the inner workings of the financial systems. They are often the only way an outside person or agency can view a company's financial information and be assured they are getting an accurate picture. Just as a child is proud to show a parent an "awesome" report card, great pride accompanies an organization with an "awesome" audit report.

1. Tell me of a time your company received an unqualified or clean (no findings) opinion on your annual financial audit report. How did this make you feel? How was this information shared with other members of your organization? How did this report reflect on the rest of your company?

2. Maybe your organization has not historically experienced the results written about in question number one. Imagine a time in the near future when you received such a glowing report. How would your company look, or be different? What steps were taken to get you to that point? How had the culture of your company changed?

3. How can you use an "awesome" audit to enhance confidence with your organization? How can you get this information to potential donors and funders in an understandable way? What might be the response?

4. An awesome audit report is just one aspect of an awesome company. The same energy that created sound financial

systems often nurtures an organization-wide culture of excellence. As a contributor to your company's excellence, how do you see your role in this culture?

76.

Technology Extending and Enhancing Our Work

In today's wired and wireless world, organizations glide when they have ample resources to stay current with the latest innovations. Technology extends the efficiency and reach of many nonprofits and simplifies many functions through automation, such as accounting, record keeping and report generation. An external audience learns about the nonprofit through the publication of books, articles and marketing materials; mailings; routing of telephone calls; solicitation of dues and donations; and online presentation of services, all of which technology enhances.

In short, technology makes it possible for nonprofits to provide more services to more recipients and more information to the general public, at lower administrative costs.

1. How does your organization best use technology? Are there other applications of technology that you especially appreciate? Why?

2. Can you tell me about a time when technology caused a breakthrough in your organization's operations or in your personal life?

3. What did it feel like to become proficient in applying the latest technology to a task you were responsible for — perhaps a task that you once did manually or by means of outdated technology?

4. Imagine that your organization had access to a technology grant to purchase hardware and/or software aimed at increasing efficiency or expanding your service offerings. What would you acquire? How would the technology improve your work and the work of colleagues?

5. How do you see the technology benefiting your recipients/members?

77.

Better Databases for Better Performance

Nonprofits are conduits; they solicit funds from members, patrons, donors, grant- makers and government agencies and use them to supply services to designated groups and the general public. They manage and balance relationships between two populations — funders and recipients/members of their services. Databases and database software simplify the management of these complex and extensive relationships and assure accurate outcome measurements for the good of the organization.

1. Describe how databases save time, money and work for you and colleagues.

2. What information do your databases provide for funders and donors? What does it have the potential to say to future donors?

3. How do your service recipients benefit from the organization having detailed and accessible information through databases?

4. If the databases were enhanced and time and data entry were not an issue, what new applications for recipient databases would you institute? If you had three wishes for improving your databases and/or processes for data entry, what would they be? Why did you make these particular choices?

5. Once granted, what would be the impact on the organization's efficiency and effectiveness?

78.

Our Numbers Define Us.

The ability to measure performance in relation to budget or objectives for service delivery provides a solid foundation for setting priorities and allocating resources. In addition, quantified outcome data influences funders. Technology makes it possible to capture, compile, analyze and display information in novel ways. Database, spreadsheet, word-processing and presentation software enable easy storage and processing of data, from which comparisons and projections can be made. By putting number and data tracking at our fingertips, these tech-tools support evaluation of the best ways to enhance services.

1. What are three things your organization measures with tech-tools that help you know you are fulfilling your mission?

2. How does performance data serve donors — the people, organizations and agencies that fund your nonprofit? How does data serve your service recipients?

3. How has your organization used performance measures to make changes that enhance the delivery of services? That improve efficiency?

4. If data collection and input were not obstacles, what new performance measures would you institute in your organization? How would capturing this data help in planning and prioritizing?

5. What ideas do you have to improve any aspect of this organization's data collection, retrieval and analysis?

136

79.

The Right Things First

In any busy organization, time is a challenge. The ability to manage ourselves, more than our time, helps us meet the demands of work. Defining which tasks are important and imperative helps prioritize activities and is the first step in getting the most important work completed first. Urgent tasks become priorities while non-essential time-wasters, such as trivia and busy work are reduced in importance and in some instances, eliminated. With practice and vigilance, concentrating on the urgent and important activities becomes the standard way you operate.

1. Tell me about a time when you had multiple projects or tasks that had similar due dates. What criteria did you use to prioritize those tasks? What made your methods successful in that what absolutely needed to get done was accomplished?

2. Given your job, tell me what you see as your most important or urgent tasks. What are some activities that distract you or get in the way of completing tasks? What skills could you develop to help curb distractions?

3. In any job, an employee's perception of priority may differ from that of her/his supervisor. Describe an instance where this was the case. What dialogue occurred that allowed for a successful result? What did you learn? How did it affect your perception of your leader?

4. Imagine you are looking two years into the future and see you have become an expert in prioritizing. You are even asked to train the staff on organization and prioritizing. What did you do to become an expert? How has this changed your work and the work of your organization? What "lessons" will you teach the staff?

Tick-Tock Time Management

Knowing how to juggle activities so that tasks are accomplished in a timely manner is a talent. Finding ways to manage time and projects, individually and throughout an organization, help ensure tasks are completed within the precious hours allotted. Creating to-do lists, utilizing project management software and knowing when you are functioning at maximum capacity, are all great ways to manage time effectively.

1. Think of a situation when you had all the time you needed to get an important project done. What did you do to make the time for this project? What worked for you in finding the time you needed? How were you able to prioritize your time?

2. At what time of day do you do your best work? How can you organize your work to take advantage of your most efficient work time?

3. What do you value about yourself when you are prioritizing your time well? How do you feel? What is the quality of your work?

4. What changes would you like to make to your time management skills for the future? What help do you need?

APPLICATIONS FOR APPRECIATIVE QUESTIONS: "LIVING" AI WITHIN YOUR NONPROFIT ORGANIZATION

Organizations have an opportunity to experience phenomenal transformation by working with the previous questions in a number of ways. By embracing the AI principles, individuals within an organization (whether or not the entire organization embraces Appreciative Inquiry) can also make a positive difference in their organization and their daily lives. This section highlights a few of the numerous ways appreciative questions can be applied to organizational processes as well as to an individual's life experiences.

Organizational Applications

1. Get meetings off to a good start. Whether you are in a staff meeting, board meeting, or community meeting, spending a few minutes posing an affirmative topic or question is a good use of time. In a larger group ask people to pair up and interview each other with a specific positive question or questions, taking turns at being the interviewer. After everyone has been interviewed, have the interviewer say a few words about what the interviewee said. Or if the group is too large, talk about the major themes they heard. In smaller groups you may go around the table asking each person to respond to a specific question to set the tone for a positive meeting. It helps if you give all members the question and a few moments to think about their answers before starting the round-robin conversation. Listen for new ideas or directions your meeting or organization might take. In future meetings begin with sharing success and accomplishment stories or highlights.

2. Alter your Human Resources practices. Peter Drucker, a renowned management theorist and author, defines leadership as "the ability to recognize and align strengths (toward a purpose) in such a way that weaknesses are irrelevant." Think about the affirmative questions you might ask in interviewing potential staff, in your performance appraisal processes and as you evaluate projects. Celebrate the positive contributions of others.

3. Implement more formal Appreciative Inquiry processes. Using the questions as the "discovery phase," you would then continue

141

through the "dream, design and destiny" phases of AI. The process contributes to transforming your organization by intentionally engaging participants in an inquiry based on positive past experiences and designing an ideal future. Continuing benefits accrue when you sustain the experience through ongoing dialogue around positive questions so everyone in the organization begins "living" the AI philosophy — looking for strengths and building on successes. Almost automatically, persons new to the organization climb aboard the AI train.

4. Conduct an Appreciative Inquiry Summit. A summit is a large group session, usually including all of an organization's internal and external stakeholders and designed to last several days. The purposes may include: starting or accelerating change; building organizational confidence; providing immediate access to information; inspiring actions; and, sustaining positive change. This book does not explicitly address summits; however The Appreciative Inquiry Summit: A Practitioner's Guide for Leading Large-Group Change is an excellent source of information.

5. Share stories you have heard. As you hear stories in your non-profit organization, what do those stories tell you about your organization's values and the way you do business? By asking appreciative questions you will begin hearing positive stories that you will want to share with others. As those stories are told, they will elicit others. Spreading positive stories enhances learning within your organization, recognizes the good work people are doing and sets a tone of appreciation that permeates the organization and into the community. Consider sharing stories in reports and presentations, newsletters, focus groups, a video, or on your website as meeting launchers and in promotional materials.

Individual Applications

You have the opportunity to be an agent of change by the questions you pose — whether you are a manager, staff person, volunteer, recipient of service, board member or donor. Those questions can be in the context of casual conversations, meetings, surveys, or reports. The work that gets done is mainly through the conversations and interactions you have with others. The following are ideas for applying positive questions in your work and thus living the Appreciative Inquiry experience.

1. Begin your day by envisioning an affirmative topic to explore. As you interact with others during the day inquire about their experiences related to your topic. Journal the themes or trends you are hearing in everyone's stories. Determine if others' experiences fit with your own experiences. What did you learn that you can apply in your own life and work? What relationships did you strengthen through your interviews?

2. Demonstrate positive intent. When tensions are running high, such as in conflict situations with board, staff, or service recipients, or serious issues arise, take a moment to reframe the situation in the positive. "Member complaint " will focus on "strategies for satisfied membership," and "low staff morale" can be addressed around "supporting and respecting employees." Ask positive questions to elicit strength building experiences and listen for and comment on possible solutions. Demonstrate a willingness to move forward together.

3. Transform "problem talk" to "possibility talk." Problem talk involves analysis of problems, determining who and what is to blame and looking backward instead of forward. When this occurs, ask a positive question to refocus the discussion on positive possibilities. For example, if someone is complaining about working conditions, ask the question, "Tell me what you would like to see here."

4. Help others enhance their strengths. Co-workers and friends are sometimes lacking in motivation due to poor self-esteem or feelings of failure. You can coach them, helping them recognize their successes and times when they felt motivated, by asking them affirmative questions. "Remember the time you led in fundraising? What were the things that put you over the top?" Listen carefully for the attitudes, relationships and habits your friend or colleague describes. Discuss how those things could be applied to presentsituations.

143

5. Keep yourself "positively charged." When you find yourself in a downward spiral in attitudes, work habits, or relationships, stop to assess how taking a positive approach might change the situation. Personally look for the "best" or most positive thing you could do that would stop a negative cycle. Ask yourself, "What opportunities for growth and learning does this situation offer?"

6. Self-reflection and continuous learning. The affirmative topics and lead-in statements provide a mini-primer of important concepts for running a successful nonprofit. Pick a topic, read the statement and then reflect on how you would answer the questions. Think about board members or several employees and how they might respond. Would there be differences? Use insights to plan how you or your organization might benefit from reconsidering some practices.

EPILOGUE: THE STORIES WE TELL...

Using affirmative, positive questions whether part of a structured Appreciative Inquiry approach or as a stand-alone process, is a potent tool for organizational and individual change. Through interviews, conversations and storytelling, the positive core values and aspirations of individuals and organizations can be articulated and changes initiated in a relatively short time frame. Of course, ongoing follow-up using positive questions and conversations is crucial for sustained success.

Designed specifically for nonprofits, this book provides examples of questions that may be used in a variety of settings and for a multitude of purposes. Each question or topic may need to be modified or expanded to fit the specific user's situation.

A logical question after reading this book is "What next? What happens after we ask the questions one-on-one or in small groups?"

Here are our suggestions for possible next steps:

- Sharing the information learned in the interviews and conversations. (data gathering)

- Identifying common themes, elements, values, experiences, etc. (analysis)

- Agreeing on a set of core values, or an engaging "provocative proposition" that all in the organization can embrace. (design)

- Establishing goals and developing action plans. (planning)

- Revisiting, reviewing and celebrating successes. (reinforcement)

This book is not designed to address all these areas. A description of the next steps can be found in the latter chapters of: The Power of Appreciative Inquiry: A Practical Guide to Positive Change by Diana Whitney and Amanda Trosten-Bloom.

There is no conclusion, or end point, to using positive questions and Appreciative Inquiry. The process of conversations is ongoing. One conversation leads to another and on and on. Through those conversations, continual insights, understandings, change, planning and commitment occur. The dynamic nonprofit organization is continually inquiring with positive and appreciative questions. In that process your organization and our world can be a better place, as our two final stories illustrate.

The last two stories are CDI's stories. They especially illuminate the power of positive inquiries to influence attitudes and activities far beyond the original target.

Funk to Fervor: Small Steps and Big Dreams

A small community — 4,000 residents — in Louisiana was notable for being one of the ten poorest areas in the country. Racially divided and economically depressed, it struggled to maintain communal identity in the face of out-migration of young people. Citizens lived with little hope and a few memories of a bygone era when the parish was comparatively prosperous. Fortunately for this town, what began as a small, Appreciative Inquiry effort building on positive conversations in one nonprofit, is now playing a major role in rekindling community spirit and planning for a more vital future.

An established local nonprofit lost substantial federal funding after years of mismanagement and deteriorating services. As a designated interim management entity, CDI enters such failing programs with the mission of enhancing their local program operations and services, providing knowledge and skills needed for staff to be competitive when new sponsors are located and helping to make the program and community a better place.

The assigned site manager recognized immediately that the organization was a microcosm of the whole community — depressed, resentful and backward-looking. Staff felt powerless to make the changes necessary to fulfill their mission. Traditional team-building techniques had proven ineffective: they produced no permanent change in attitudes or interactions and when staff members talked, no one appeared to listen.

The new manager had experienced Appreciative Inquiry through CDI. Although she did not possess formal training in AI, she saw the possibility of using it to animate her disheartened organization. Arranging a staff retreat, she used positive questions to encourage staff to talk about what really mattered to them. The energy generated during and immediately after the retreat was infectious.
Subsequently, other AI processes were introduced throughout the agency. The results had an impact not only on the agency but also influenced neighborhood and community improvement actions.

One of the staff's biggest complaints: "people aren't being heard" — was in fact shorthand for a style of communication characterized by rumor, gossip, innuendo, complaints and opinion-mongering. Through using AI, "provocative propositions" — *statements of possibility* — were developed to insure positive communication became the norm. The site manager described the resulting change this way: "When I came to the organization, one of the first things I noticed was silence, uncanny silence, as if people had given up talking to one another. Now when I walk around, I hear the hum of conversation in every corner of our offices. To me, it's the sound of happiness from people engaging in activities that make a difference."

A mental health consultant, who has worked with the children's program over a number of years, recently reported compelling accounts showing significant positive changes in staff interactions with children and the children's behavior and development. A precipitous drop in problem behaviors in the classrooms occurred as teachers became happier working there and enthusiastically sought out classes to increase their professional skills.

From the start, the organization's connection to the community was an issue due to the many years it neglected its clients. As the use of AI had an immediate beneficial impact on how the organization functioned internally, it soon resulted in positive impacts for its immediate neighborhood. A case in point: broken and unsafe equipment, installed in the 1950's, made up a dilapidated playground adjacent to the agency. Through community organization and donations, a local architect created a site plan, hazardous equipment was removed and a "yard party" cleared the ground, built a sandbox, installed a barbeque and brought in movable playthings: tricycles, wagons, outdoor building blocks. Eventually, permanent and safe playground equipment will be installed.

Unexpectedly, an opportunity to benefit the community at large arose. A new billboard reading *New Voice — New Vision* appeared one day: the newly elected mayor's promise to the people. The mayor wanted to create a vibrant and cohesive community — one like the older residents described in compelling stories of the past.

Recognizing yet another application for AI, the site manager met with the mayor, described how her organization was reinventing itself and asked to collaborate with him on applying these ideas toward community renewal. The mayor enthusiastically accepted her partnership and convened a small group of twenty civic leaders and opinion-makers for a town meeting. The meeting included interviews using positive questions. As a result participants discovered that they wanted the same thing — to restore their community. They each had many different, but interesting, ideas about how to get there.

The mayor seized the opportunity of bringing people together to discuss community affairs in a positive, strength-based context as the path to renewal and has scheduled ongoing town meetings to talk and plan. Residents are enthused. One result is a local ministry began operating a new coffee shop, conceived of as a cozy place for townsfolk to gather and have conversations. Some of these conversations are undoubtedly about exciting possibilities for the future.

Authors' Story: Ours is a great place to work, however, sometimes...

Community Development Institute (CDI), an established, successful nonprofit organization, prides itself on high employee involvement in planning, setting policy, developing effective self-directed teams and managing projects. CDI employees consistently report feeling supported and appreciated. But even a values-driven organization like ours, committed to creating a life-enhancing workplace, occasionally stumbles.

Although producing exceptional results, challenges recently beset our 15-member finance department. All members have ongoing accountability for managing multi-million dollar budgets in a variety of programs around the country where CDI provides interim leadership and management. They also must coordinate internally with CDI program administrators and externally with fiscal officers in the local community programs. This necessitates an autonomous, professional and responsible staff having good communication skills on several levels.

However, unusual circumstances diverted their attention from their usually high quality work. First, two staff members were terminated. Shortly after that, only a few people from the finance department were included in a training program that took place in a very desirable setting. Although training participants were chosen on the basis of relevance to responsibilities, those selected were perceived as privileged. Rumblings developed among department staff and began to seep into other areas in the organization.

Identifying strengths and building on successes are values we embrace. So we suppressed our impulse to call a meeting to justify our decisions about the terminations and training participants. We chose instead to tap our employees "positive core" — the identification of what *is* and what *has been* best, their living values and positive potential. By adopting an Appreciative Inquiry approach, we engaged staff in one-on-one interviews using positive, affirmative questions as the starting point for a dialogue leading to plans for enhancing the work environment. Conversations ensued around the following questions:

- Describe your peak positive experience in the finance department since coming to work for CDI. What made it a peak experience?
- What was your contribution to this experience?
- How did others contribute to making it a peak experience?

149

- What core values were present in your and others' contributions?
- How could we make this department even better?

The word "problem" never crossed our lips. Instead we focused on "opportunities," using past successes to create our future. By sharing stories, identifying core values and talking about ways to create a more supportive work environment, staff rebuilt relationships and reinforced the understandings of their purpose; all within one morning meeting.

The commitment and energy generated through this structured conversation continues to produce affirmative results. Being determined to build on the energy and enthusiasm the brief inquiry produced, two members of our finance team were asked to design and lead a follow-up Appreciative Inquiry. A meeting of the finance staff, scheduled for 90 minutes, turned into an entire morning of constructive, upbeat conversation, leading to the formulation of action plans endorsed by the entire finance team.

The morning began with brainstorming a question about the values that underlie the department's commitment to producing high-quality work for internal and external clients. The following is an excerpt from the summary of the initial brainstorming session:

> CDI's financial team is unique in the work we do and in the nature of our operations. We serve both CDI and numerous Head Start and other clients throughout the country. ... Our job is to put their financial house in order. In the conduct of our enterprise, we exemplify CDI's values of community, fiscal responsibility, stewardship of funds, direct and open communication and extraordinary leadership at all levels.

The leaders broadened the inquiry to elicit staff members' positive personal experiences, feelings and ideas about how to enhance services and responsiveness to both internal and external customers. How do we work more effectively as a team? Three small workgroups developed and presented their clever, thought provoking displays reflecting a Miracle Team: the team composition, the nature of the team's work, how it would feel to play on the team and the everyday practices supporting it.

Themes that emerged:

- Everyone on the team contributes and is acknowledged for his or her contribution.
- Team members strike a balance between their work and home lives.
- Each person works autonomously and self-reliantly, *while* teamwork offers mutual support.

The charge for the group as the morning drew to a close was translating these widely held, affirmative understandings into actions that would make the department's work more fulfilling, both professionally and personally. Collectively, the group adopted a few everyday practices:

- Offer and ask for help.
- Provide ongoing professional education and cross-training.
- Take initiative to make things happen.

Specific activities developed to achieve these practices included:

- Engage in biweekly check-ins to acknowledge how team members have used their teams to support them in their autonomous accountabilities. The routine of holding check-ins took hold slowly but has gathered steam as the habit of offering and asking for help has been established.
- Bring fun to the workplace: hold monthly potlucks during office hours to acknowledge birthdays and achievements choose "wellness buddies" to support healthy lifestyles, schedule off-hours activities like bowling that may include friends and family.
- Ask senior management to make recommended structural changes to enhance departmental operations. Management's responsiveness to this request boosted morale even more.
- Schedule training in techniques for communication and other

151

requested topics.
- Each financial specialist will seek feedback from his/her internal and external clients through a customer-satisfaction survey, composed of positive questions.

The meeting, conducted in accordance with AI principles, reinforced staff members' resolve to approach their work from an appreciative, strengths-based perspective. One staff member summed up the impact of the meeting as follows:

> "Before the meeting, I think our big complaint about the department was that there wasn't much connection between us. One of the hardest things for us to overcome was cynicism — our belief that there was nothing we could do to affect our experience of the workplace and the performance of the department. The AI process helped us to see that we can influence what happens and be accountable for it, as individuals and as a team."

The AI processes used within our fiscal department influenced the entire organization. As people began to talk and envision a more positive and productive work environment, unpredicted changes evolved:
- A wellness program evolved where staff selected "wellness buddies" to enhance motivation and commitment to new life skills.
- A newly established Human Resources Team, most of whom have functions other than human resources, addressed implementing ideas and activities to extend the finance department's vision of a friendly, supportive and fun environment into the entire organization.
- Financial reporting structures and reports were simplified to make them more user friendly to the non-financial CDI staff.
- Streamlined reporting and tracking systems facilitated comprehensive billing procedures to capture all possible revenue, benefiting everyone.
- Spontaneously, playtimes, potlucks, celebrations and acknowledgments became an important part of CDI's culture.

152

With support from its leadership, CDI continues working tirelessly to "live and be" AI, creating a positive, energetic work environment, fostering outstanding work and constantly regenerating the atmosphere to practice AI on an ongoing basis.

You have read just a few of thousands of stories being told that illustrate the power of posing positive questions and the transformations possible within nonprofit organizations and individuals.

FOR OTHER STORIES AND IDEAS PLEASE VISIT THE WEBSITE:
http://appreciativeinquiry.cwru.edu.

It is a wonderful and inspiring forum for exchange of successful applications of Appreciative Inquiry and getting answers to your questions.

"I have seen over and over again — all around the world — what happens when people who are not used to being valued feel heard. The experience of being heard allows them to be present and to offer the best of themselves in a way that could not happen otherwise."

–The Reverend Canon Charles P. Gibbs; United Religions Initiative

Organizations as Networks of Conversation:
An Emerging Model of Organizational Theory

The stories in this book and in all the Appreciative Inquiry (AI) texts are testament to the near-inevitability of powerful results where AI is systematically used for organizational transformation. The AI approach is deceptively simple: people have the power to change their organizations for the better by articulating, emphasizing and acting upon their positive aspects: through words and actions.

This appendix presents some implications of AI and the history of organizational thought so the reader can place the stories and texts in a theoretical and experiential context. A new model of organizational theory is emerging from the successful experiments of hundreds of AI practitioners using the power of positive questions; old models of organizations do not illuminate what is taking place in these extraordinary transformational experiences. Nor do the previous models provide theoretical guidance for moving organizations beyond asking positive questions into sustaining new directions. The new model, emphasizing sustainability, draws from the work of AI theorists (particularly Michael Mantel and Jim Ludema), positive psychologists, social constructionists, and the ground-breaking work of organizations such as Landmark Education.

In the course description for its two-day workshop, Communication: Access to Power, Landmark Education says,

"…when we see language and communication as both that

155

which give rise to the world and also as the instruments that give us access to everything in that world, it alters the very nature of what is possible in our lives [and in our organizations]. Communication and language then come to be seen for what they are, creative acts."

These powerful words are at the heart of what becomes possible when organizations are viewed as Networks of Conversation. Transformation that is rapid, deep and lasting — for both organizations as a whole and for the people who comprise them — results from adopting and acting on this perspective.

To understand the power and limitations of a particular theory on the speed, quality and scope of an organizational change process, we must understand the two most influential theoretical models that have informed most organizational thought over the last century — Scientific Management and Sociotechnical Systems.

Scientific Management – Organization as Machine

A relatively young field, organization theory began with the ideas informing the design of assembly line manufacturing plants in this country. During the first half of the twentieth century the model for organizations was the very machine they produced. A mechanistic theory of how organizations functioned best, "Scientific Management" maintained machines and the organizations that produce them are composed of many parts sequentially arranged each with its own separate critical role.

This theory focused on the technology, tools and knowledge required to produce a product. According to the theory, when these parts were scientifically assembled by technical engineers the proper functioning of the machine or organization could be assured. When a part (person, technology or piece of equipment) was not functioning properly it was replaced and the machine was put back to work.

Scientific Management focused on the internal physical work flow with little thought given to the impact the process design had on the people in the work force. With craftsmanship considered a relic, a worker was merely a pair of hands, having checked his/her brains at

156

the door — prerequisites for surviving a mechanistic atmosphere. A perfectible machine replaced an imperfect human being. To eliminate the possibility for human error, jobs were reduced to their simplest motions, and individuals were assigned routine tasks. People were expected to behave in the same manner as the machines their organizations produced. Innovations and improvements were incremental at best, with many plants retaining the same processes and organizational structures, which produced minimally acceptable quality for decades. Hierarchical, top-down control prevailed. Proposed changes filtered through a multi-layered decision-making process before official adoption. Directors and managers made decisions, based on the technical knowledge of engineers, with no input from the people doing the work, let alone the customer.

Though its limitations are now obvious, Scientific Management was largely responsible for tremendous accomplishments in quality standardization and predictable productivity. It made consumer goods affordable; it established the economic superiority of the United States during the twentieth century. This view of organizations was unchallenged until the advent of "quality circles" enabled Japanese manufacturers to threaten some of America's most dominating industries in the early 1980's. Although quality circles were, for the most part, implemented within the framework of Scientific Management principles and traditional top down control, they did foster increased worker participation, made workplaces more human and improved the quality of work.

Sociotechnical Systems – An Organization as a Living Organism

Fundamental change — away from Scientific Management to a more powerful theory of organizations — started in Europe. Beginning in the early 1950's, the view of organizations as machines began to shift with the groundbreaking study by Trist and Bamforth on the effects of mechanization in British coal mines. Their work revealed that the productivity, quality, morale and other industrial problems arising when new technology was introduced, came from inadequate attention to the social structure and human requirements of those working in the organization. Organizational effectiveness was not simply a function

157

of the factory's technical system or, for that matter, the factory's social system (as some in the human relations movement who focused primarily on worker satisfaction argued). Rather, a successful organization depended on the optimal interaction of both systems. Through their work with the Norwegian Industrial Democracy Project in the early 1960's, Eric Trist and Fred Emery developed this new organizational model.

The theory and approach to organizational transformation was called Sociotechnical Systems (STS), which emphasized the relationships between the human interactions of an organization and the technical workflow. STS are based on the concept that work can be more satisfying and productive if teams are organized around whole tasks and have responsibility for accomplishing those tasks. Organization development movements, such as human relations, team training, and even quality circles, focused on worker satisfaction as the route to organizational effectiveness. STS analysis always focused on task performance and enhanced overall organizational effectiveness, with greatly enhanced satisfaction a fortuitous byproduct.

STS represented a reaction to and a fundamental break from Scientific Management's top down control orientation and dehumanizing characteristics by integrating the human (social) and technical (tools) systems. In doing so, it put work along with the freedom and power to innovate, back into the worker's hands — as it had been during the age of artisans and craftsmen, before the industrial revolution.

Organizations designed on STS principles also developed the capacity for adaptation, innovation and responsiveness to external circumstances which is the definition of a living organism. Hence, STS is sometimes called the "living organism theory" of organizations.

The whole system is made up of people (the social system) using tools, techniques, processes and knowledge (the technical system) to produce goods or services valued by customers, regulated by government and supplied with raw materials by vendors (who are part of the organization's external environment). How well the social and technical systems are designed, with respect to one another and to the demands of the external environment, determine the organization's effectiveness.

STS includes these dimensions:

- Individual and team job design form a whole-system approach that breaks down barriers between departments. Implicit in this model is the idea: If you want people to do a good job, you need to give them a good job to do.
- Meaningful work, whether individual or team based, must include such critical core dimensions as skill variety, task identity and task significance.
- Individuals and teams require a certain level of autonomy to complete their tasks as well as receiving feedback on the quality of their work. These factors nurture workforce responsibility for outcomes and provide information on how the team's work impacts the whole organization. The final result is vastly increased organizational effectiveness, as well as worker satisfaction.

Shortcomings in applying this organizational theory were that STS redesign projects were often costly and time consuming (the period from management commitment, through systems analysis, design, training and finally implementation often stretched 18 months or more); manager and employee resistance to change often blocked a design team's efforts; directors were sometimes impatient with the learning curve of teams; and employee suspicions of managers sometimes stood in the way of building effective management/employee partnerships. Although STS redesign involves representatives of, and input from workers and customers, comprehensive participation in the change process has not generally occurred. Nonetheless, experimentation with STS redesign over the last 50 years has produced extraordinary breakthroughs in organizational effectiveness along with improved customer and workforce satisfaction.

Appreciative Inquiry – The Organization as Networks of Conversation

Since its inception, AI has tapped something different as the source of organizational transformation. AI is not scientific or mechanistic, nor based on analyses of systems, structures or environmental influences, nor dependent on team or management training. Instead, AI's power flows from intentional conversations among people as the source for transformation, opening untapped reserves of energy, commitment, productivity, and creativity and nurtures the warmth of human relationships in the workplace.

AI is an organizational framework for engaging in purposeful conversations about strengths and core values in a way that makes sense of when and how an organization functions best. The organization's participants interview each other based on questions designed to identify the organization's positive core.

Describing organizations as Networks of Conversation implies far more than an organization's culture — its norms for behavior. Looking at the recurring patterns of communication in an organization reveals that these conversational networks continuously shape an organization, determining what is possible and what is not, focusing on the future not the past. Networks of Conversation constitute the source and energy behind all of organizational life. AI's organizational theory stretches beyond either the machine or the living organism as a metaphor for an organization by assuming that organizations, at their core, are Networks of Conversation. The daily use of language among people breathes life into the organization. The content, quality and intentionality of the ongoing conversations provide energy, forward direction, vitality and success.

Through intentional conversation, new possibilities immediately open — some in a matter of minutes or hours as opposed to months or years. Hundreds of organizations engaged in the AI process have experienced a dramatic shift from negativity, doubts, concerns, problem orientation with a past-based focus, to energetic optimism, creativity and new and greater possibilities. Structured positive questions leading participants into conversations that identify strengths and values move an organization immediately and radically away from problem solving, faultfinding and analysis of past mistakes toward a powerful positive future focus.

When fully implemented, these unique principles, the spoken language with its interplay of ideas and emotions, provides a spark — an instantaneous rewiring of internal circuits that supersedes past fixed ways of thinking and being for individuals and organizations. In short,

160

through conversations, human beings can generate raw energy, renewed purpose and transformation for themselves and their organizations.

Can the initial burst of energy and creativity be sustained? After all, in nature, natural systems tend toward entropy and without intentional intervention; social systems tend toward dissonance and cacophony. By intentionally and continuously focusing on the most powerful aspirations of individual members and the organization as a whole, positive change in social systems can be sustained. Through face to face (or at least voice to voice) dialogue, the process remains alive and vital.

A key component of a sustained AI process is appreciative leadership, which means an ongoing individual commitment to engage others, to recognize that all people have intrinsic worth, to value their strengths, to ask positive questions engaging others and to first imagine and then construct positive futures. Appreciative leadership cements such a powerful alliance on emphasizing strengths in such a way that weaknesses become irrelevant. This is not a "Pollyanna" approach. It is challenging; confronting hard work requiring leaders to continuously reinvent themselves as beacons of possibility. The core of appreciative change is leadership's belief in the goal of what's possible and the courage to continually bring it forward by engaging rather than avoiding conflict, living with the uncertainty of outcomes, and most importantly confidently believing in collectively creating something better by including all stakeholders.

Continuous broad based stakeholder participation in the conversations which shape an organization is a radical concept. It not only shifts power relationships, but also generates ongoing enthusiasm by engaging everyone at all levels in the organization. By pushing the decision-making point as far out from the central leadership as possible, Appreciative Inquiry, encourages self-management practices and decentralized decision-making, liberates local, smaller unit staff to innovate, and energizes their strengths, assets and resources. While demonstrating responsiveness to local initiatives, appreciative leadership offers support which simultaneously balances openness with organizational focus on big picture goals.

161

Thus, appreciative leaders incorporate appreciative design elements into all their organizational structures. They do this by remaining open to a shared vision and collective goal-setting; developing themselves as appreciative leaders; intentionally creating structures that include all organization members; and being committed to systematic appreciative inquiries into the organization's positive core — that which gives it viability and strength. In sum, after the initial launch, an organization's leadership needs to be vigilant about providing "booster shots" for appreciative interventions through continuous, intentional shaping of the Networks of Conversation that form the heart, soul and core of every organization.

A Brief Overview of the Appreciative Inquiry Process

What is Appreciative Inquiry?

Appreciative inquiry is an approach to organization change that has been used successfully in small and large change projects with hundreds of organizations worldwide. It is based on the simple idea that organizations move in the direction of what they ask questions about. For example, when groups study human problems and conflicts, they often find that both the number and severity of these problems grow. In the same way, when groups study high human ideals and achievements, such as peak experiences, best practices and noble accomplishments, these phenomena, too, tend to flourish. Thus, Appreciative Inquiry distinguishes itself from other change methodologies by deliberately asking *positive questions* to ignite constructive dialogue and inspired action within organizations.

How to Use Appreciative Inquiry

As a method of organizational intervention, Appreciative Inquiry differs from traditional problem-solving approaches. The basic assumption of problem-solving methodologies is that people and organizations are fundamentally "broken" and need to be fixed. The process usually involves: (1) identifying the key problems; (2) analyzing the root causes; (3) searching for possible solutions; and (4) developing an action plan.

In contrast, the underlying assumption of Appreciative Inquiry is that people and organizations are by nature full of assets, capabilities, resources and strengths that are just waiting to be located, affirmed, stretched and encouraged. The steps include: (1) discovering and valuing; (2) envisioning; (3) design through dialogue; and (4) co-constructing the future. In other words, the Appreciative Inquiry 4-D model includes discovery, dream, design and delivery.

Appreciative Inquiry is an approach to organizational analysis and learning that is uniquely intended for discovering, understanding and fostering innovations in social organizational arrangements and processes. Appreciative Inquiry refers to both a search for knowledge and a theory of intentional collective action, which are designed to evolve the vision and will of a group, organization or society as a whole. It is an inquiry process that affirms our symbolic capacities of imagination and mind as well as our social capacity for conscious choice and cultural evolution. The art of appreciation is the art of discovering and valuing those factors that give life to an organization or group. The process involves interviewing and storytelling to draw the best of the past to set the stage for effective visualization of what might be.

Perspectives

Inquiry into "the art of the possible" in organizational life should begin with appreciation. Every system works to some degree and a primary task of management and organizational analysis is to discover, describe and explain those "exceptional moments" which give life to the system and activate members' competencies and energies. The appreciative approach takes its inspiration from "what is." Valuing, learning and inspired understanding – these are the aims of the appreciative spirit.

Inquiry into what's possible should be applicable. Organizational study should lead to the generation of knowledge that can be used, applied and validated in action.

Inquiry into what's possible should be provocative. An organization is an open-ended, indeterminate system capable of: becoming more than it is at any given moment and, learning how to actively take part in guiding its own evolution. Appreciative knowledge of "what is" becomes provocative to the extent that the learning takes on a normative value for members. In this way Appreciative Inquiry allows us to use systematic management analysis to help the organization's members shape an effective future according to their own imaginative and moral purposes.

Inquiry into the human potential of organizational life should be collaborative. This principle assumes an inseparable relationship between the process of inquiry and its content. A unilateral approach to the study of social innovation is a direct negation of the phenomenon itself.

Appreciative Inquiry seeks out the exceptional best of "what is" to help ignite the collective imagination of "what might be." The aim is to generate new knowledge, which expands "the realm of the possible" and helps members of an organization envision a collectively desired future and to carry forth that vision in ways which successfully translate images into possibility, intentions into reality and belief into practice.

First, you *discover and value* those factors that give life to the organization. The challenge of valuing is to discover, for example, the commitment of the organization and to find out when that commitment was its highest. Regardless of how few the moments of highest commitment, the task is to zero in on these and to discuss the factors and forces that created the possibility for them. The list of positive or affirmative topics for discovery is endless: high quality, integrity, empowerment, innovation, customer responsiveness, technological innovation, team spirit, etc. In each case the task is discovery of the positive exceptions, successes and most vital or alive effective moments. Discovery involves valuing those things of value worth valuing. And it can be done both within and across organizations (in a bench marking sense) and across time ("organizational history as positive possibility").

Second, you *envision* what might be. When the best of what is has been identified, the mind naturally begins to search beyond this; it begins to envision new possibilities. Valuing the best of what it needs to envisioning what might be. Envisioning involves "passionate thinking" – it means creating a positive image of a desired and preferred future.

Third, you engage in *dialogue*. This is simply the open sharing of discoveries and possibilities. Through dialogue, a consensus begins to emerge whereby individuals in the organization say, "Yes this is an ideal or vision that we value and should aspire to." It is through

The Nonprofits' Guide to the Power of Appreciative inquiry

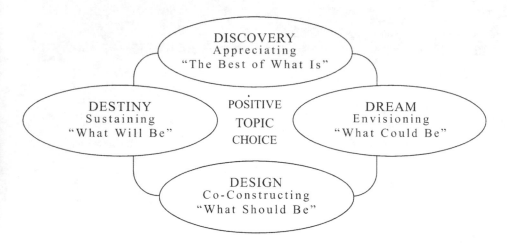

dialogue that individual appreciation becomes collective appreciation; individual will evolves into group will; and individual vision becomes a cooperative or **shared** vision for the organization. Appreciative Inquiry helps create a deliberately supportive context for dialogue. It is through the sharing of ideals that social bonding occurs.

Fourth, you *construct the future* through innovation and action. Appreciative Inquiry establishes momentum of its own. Members of the organization find innovative ways to help move the organization closer to the ideal. **Because the ideals are grounded in realities, there is the confidence to try to make things happen.** This is important to underscore because it is precisely because of the visionary content, placed in juxtaposition to grounded examples of the extraordinary, that Appreciative Inquiry opens the status quo to transformations in collective action. By seeking an imaginative and fresh perception of organizations, as if seen for the very first time, the appreciative eye takes nothing for granted, searching to apprehend the basis of organizational life and working to articulate those possibilities, giving witness to a better existence.

For more information on Appreciative Inquiry, please see our bibliography.

BIBLIOGRAPHY

Buckingham, Marcus and Clifton, Donald O. Now, Discover Your Strengths. New York: The Free Press, 2001.

Buckingham, Marcus and Coffman, Curt. First, Break all the Rules: What the World's Greatest Managers Do Differently. New York: Simon & Schuster, 1999.

Cooperrider, David L. and Whitney, Diana. Collaborating for Change: Appreciative Inquiry. San Francisco, CA: Berrett-Koehler, 1999.

Covey, Stephen R. The 7 Habits of Highly Effective People. New York: Simon & Schuster, 1989.

Drucker, Peter F. The Five Most Important Questions You Will Ever Ask About Your Nonprofit Organization. San Francisco, CA: Jossey-Bass, 1993.

Gillham, Jane (Editor.) Science of Optimism and Hope: Research Essays in Honor of Martin E.P. Seligman. Philadelphia: Templeton Foundation Press, 2000.

Goleman, Daniel, McKee, Annie and Boyatzis, Richard E. Primal Leadership: Realizing the Power of Emotional Intelligence. Boston: Harvard Business School Press, 2002.

Ludema, James., Whitney, Diana., Mohr, Bernard J. and Griffin Thomas J. The Appreciative Inquiry Summit: A Practitioner's Guide for Leading Large-Group Change. San Francisco, CA: Berrett-Koehler, 2003.

Mantel, M. & Ludema, J. 2004. " Sustaining Appreciative Change: Inviting Conversational Convergence Through Relational Leadership and Organizational Design". Advances in Appreciative Inquiry. Volume 1. Cooperrider, D. and Avital, M. Oxford, UK: Elsevier Ltd.

Nelson, J. G. Six Keys to Recruiting, Orienting and Involving

NonProfit Board Members. Washington D.C.: National Center for Nonprofit Boards, second printing 1995.

Seligman, Martin. Learned Optimism: How to Change Your Mind and Your Life New York: Simon & Schuster, 1998.

Snyder, C.R. (Editor) and Lopez, Shane J. (Editor.) Handbook of Positive Psychology. London: Oxford University Press, 2002.

Wheatley, Margaret J. Turning to One Another: simple conversations to restore hope to the future. San Francisco, CA: Berrett-Koehler, 2002.

Whitney, Diana, Cooperrider, David L., Trosten-Bloom, Amanda. and Kaplin, Brian S. Encyclopedia of Positive Questions – Volume One: Using Appreciative Inquiry to Bring out the Best in Your Organization. Euclid, OH: Lakeshore, 2002.

Whitney, Diana. and Trosten-Bloom, Amanda. The Power of Appreciative Inquiry – A Practical Guide to Positive Change. San Francisco, CA: Berrett-Koehler, 2003.

Community Development Institute (CDI) was established as a nonprofit organization in 1970 to provide training, technical assistance, organizational development and management services to public agencies and private organizations and groups. CDI's mission is to inspire people and communities to generate their own transformation. CDI is a nationally recognized leader in redesigning organizations and developing high-performance teams. CDI has worked effectively with major corporations (Kodak, Corning, R. R. Donnelley & Sons, Pacific Gas and Electric), the U.S. Department of Health and Human Services, the IRS, the U.S. Navy, the U.S. Forest Service, state agencies and nonprofit organizations. In the last three decades, CDI has successfully managed over $100 million in contracts, grants and cooperative agreements — primarily through funding from the U.S. Department of Health and Human Services.

CDI staff engages in its own continuous improvement processes that foster CDI's organizational excellence. CDI works from a shared vision and mission, in an environment conducive to knowledge exchange, creativity and collaborative planning and problem-solving. CDI operates with a view to rigorous financial and administrative accountability. On all projects, CDI establishes safeguard systems for responsible use of government and private funds. Dun & Bradstreet rates CDI "strong" for financial management.

The Nonprofits' Guide to the Power of Appreciative inquiry

For More Information on Appreciative Inquiry Consulting for Your Organization *or* To Purchase Additional Copies of This Book Contact CDI at:

EMAIL: info@cditeam.org
PHONE: 1-800-488-2348
WEB: www.cditeam.org
MAIL: 9745 E. Hampden, Suite 310
Denver, CO 80231

172